FreeStuff

FOR

Pet Lovers

ON THE INTERNET

GLORIA HANSEN

C&T PUBLISHING

Developmental Editor: Barbara Kuhn
Cover and Book Design: Christina Jarumay
Book Production: Nancy Koerner
Production Coordination: Diane Pedersen
Production Assistant: Stephanie Muir

Library of Congress Cataloging-in-Publication Data

Hansen, Gloria.
    Free stuff for pet lovers on the Internet / Gloria Hansen.
        p.   cm.
    ISBN 1-57120-124-6 (paper trade)
    1. Pets--Computer network resources--Directories. 2. Internet
addresses--Directories. 3. Free material. I. Title.
    SF411.5 .H375 2001
    025.06'6360887--dc21

                                        00-012511

Published by C&T Publishing, Inc.
P.O. Box 1456
Lafayette, California 94549

Printed in China
10   9   8   7   6   5   4   3   2   1

DEDICATION

In loving memory of my dad, Robert J. Patrowicz.

ACKNOWLEDGEMENTS

My deepest thanks to all of the pet lovers who share so generously of themselves and their wisdom on the Web; without you, this book would not be possible.

My heartfelt thanks to my husband, Richard Hansen, for bringing Mustang into our lives, and to Dr. Michael R. Petranto, Chris Schweickert, and the dedicated staff at the East Windsor Animal Hospital who tirelessly give extraordinary care to animals—and to their often frantic owners.

My gratitude to Christina Jarumay for graciously adding an illustration of my dog to this cover and for her awesome cover artwork on all the Free Stuff books, and to Barb Kuhn and the team at C&T Publishing for their continued guidance and support.

DEAR READER,

Sifting through thousands of the sites to create this book was a challenge. My goal was to include sites that will be updated with fresh information and offer the best advice and guidance for pet lovers. That doesn't mean, however, there aren't many more sites out there that are equally illuminating and valuable; you will find others. Given the fluid nature of the Web, it is possible that some of the sites in this book may move or even vanish. Even so, I believe this book gives you the needed tools to help you navigate the vast, ever-evolving world known as the Web. Enjoy the ride. —Gloria

SYMBOLS IN THIS BOOK

While you can find lots of valuable information on the Internet, you can learn more by joining in some of the many discussion groups offered on the Web. This icon indicates that the site offers some type of forum you can join.

 This icon signifies extra-special advice.

When you see this icon, read carefully. It represents hard-earned wisdom—something I probably learned the hard way.

This icon tells you that the Web site sells merchandise related to the free information that they offer.

Table of Contents

join the Pet Lovers' Fun on the Web!

Pet lovers are special people who wholeheartedly understand the human-animal bond. Spot, Skipper, and Fluffy aren't merely pets, but deeply loved members of the family. Pet lovers flock to the Web to chat about their furry, feathered, and finned friends. They know the Web is the place where a cornucopia of pet-related information and answers reign. Wondering if you can take Skipper along to a bed & breakfast in Maine? Tap into **Pets Welcome** to find out. Pondering which dog breed is right for your family? Read insightful articles at **PETsMART.com** for guidance. Puzzled whether to shave your thick-furred Husky in the summer? Visit **Healthy Pets** for direction. No matter the question, chances are you'll find the answer on the Web—and this book will show you the way.

THIS BOOK WILL HELP YOU USE THE WEB TO QUICKLY LOCATE THE BEST FREE INFORMATION FOR PET LOVERS.

A few years ago you could type almost any question into a Web search engine, such as **Altavista** (**http://www.altavsita.com**), and find an answer with a few quick clicks. Today it's not so easy. The Web has become the world's largest library, and its plethora of unorganized sites can be overwhelming. Using a search engine can turn up thousands of results—a mosaic of the helpful and the not-so-helpful, and often the not-so-useful. Yet, with this book in hand, you will save valuable time by quickly locating the best Web sites for your needs. This book shows you how to get on the Web and quickly find:

- The biggest and best pet-related Web sites where you'll read feature stories, the latest news, and solutions to your pet concerns.
- Chat groups and bulletin boards where you can post pet-related questions and get answers—sometimes within minutes.
- Web sites with directories of pet shelters and adoption agencies.
- Web sites offering pet-friendly travel guidance.
- Web sites with the best pet care, behavior, and training help.
- Web sites where you can listen to pet radio shows.

AMERICA ONLINE IS GREAT FOR BEGINNERS

America Online is a commercial online service that offers original content and a gateway to the Internet. It's very easy to install, making it a great choice for beginners. If you are not one of the millions who received an AOL special-offer CD in the mail or found one falling from the pages of a favorite magazine, you can request a free AOL installation CD by calling 1-800/827-6364. Or, if you know someone with Internet access, you can ask them to download you a copy of the software from AOL's Web site (**http://www.aol.com**). AOL offers different pricing plans, from $4.95 for limited monthly access to $21.95 for unlimited access.

To install AOL on your computer, load the CD, click the install icon, and follow the instructions. The program helps locate your closest access number (the number your program will dial to get you online) and configures your computer settings (great for those who'd rather not tinker with settings). Within a short matter of time, you're online hearing "Welcome." While online, take the offered tour to understand how AOL works and what it offers. You'll quickly discover why AOL has millions of subscribers—it's fun and offers plenty of organized, easy-to-follow content.

However, AOL may add surcharges in addition to their fees. For example, if there is no local access number to AOL in your area, you may be charged for long distance calls by your telephone company (in addition to AOL's fees) for the next closest number. Or if you use an AOL 800 access number, AOL will add a surcharge of monthly bill of $6.00 per hour of use to your monthly bill.

AOL KEYWORDS

```
[▼][pets                                              ][ Go ][ Search ][Keyword]
```

Keywords are shortcuts that allow you to jump to different places on AOL. To access the AOL's pets area using a keyword, type **Pets** into the white navigation box on AOL's toolbar (where it says, "Type Search words, Keywords or Web Addresses here"), and click the **go** button.

You can also type keywords into AOL's keyword box. Click the keyword box icon on the AOL's navigation toolbar, or press **Ctrl-K** (or ⌘**-K** on a Mac).

✋ *It's confusing when you type in what you think is an AOL keyword, only to have AOL's browser whisk you to the Web. This happens because keywords can also be used in place of long web addresses, or to start an Internet search. To tell whether you're in AOL or on the Web, look at the white navigation box on AOL's toolbar. If it has a URL address in it (for example:* **http://www.somewhereontheweb.com***), you're on the Web. If it says "Type Search words, Keywords or Web Addresses here," you're still in AOL.*

HOW TO USE AMERICA ONLINE'S WEB BROWSER

To jump from AOL to a Web site, you simply need to type the Web site's URL (Uniform Resource Locator—the Web site's address) into the white navigation box on AOL's toolbar and click the **go** button.

For example, if you type <**http://www.petsmart.com**>, AOL's Web browser window will open with the **PETsMART.com** site.

To jump from the Web site back to a favorite place you visited on AOL, mouse-click and hold on the arrow button to the left of the white navigation box on the toolbar. This will display a drop-down menu that lists the last 25 places you visited— either on the Web or on AOL. To return to a favorite place, simply select it from this list.

Learn More about AOL and Stay Safe on AOL.

While connected to AOL, start with Keyword: **Help** for a good overview of the service. Keyword: **Customer Service** provides information on 24-hour help services and keywords to other helpful areas. Visit Keyword: **Neighborhood Watch**, Keyword: **Official Mail**, and see the general Web safety tips later in this chapter for more information on staying safe while online.

Head to Keyword:
Help Community
for message boards
loaded with excel-
lent tech support,
free online classes
on AOL and the
Internet, and plenty
of hints and tips.

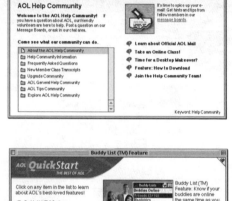

Keyword: **Best of**
AOL *is filled with*
tips and tutorials
for using AOL's
most popular fea-
tures such as the
buddy list and
Instant Message
conversations.

Visit Keyword:
Neighborhood
Watch *for informa-*
tion on parental
controls, e-mail
safety, computer
safety, and suggest-
ed safeguards.

Never give any personal information, such as your password or credit card numbers, to anyone. If you receive a request for any personal information, do not respond. Instead, report it to AOL. See Keyword: **Notify** for guidance.

AOL only sends its Official Mail to users within a blue envelope with a blue border that includes the official AOL seal. When you view the e-mail, you'll notice a light-blue border behind the mail buttons, and the official AOL seal located on the lower left corner of the mail border. Note that AOL will never ask you for your password or other personal information.

T I P

The white navigation box on the AOL toolbar indicates whether you are on AOL or on the Web.

`▼ Type Search words, Keywords or Web Addresses here     Go   Search  Keyword`

If you see "Type Search words, Keywords or Web Addresses here" in the white box, you're on AOL.

`▼ http://www.petsmart.com     Go   Search  Keyword`

If you see a URL address, such as **http://www.petsmart.com**, you're on the Web.

FINDING PET-RELATED FUN ON AMERICA ONLINE

To access AOL's Pets main area, type the Keyword: **Pets**. You'll find a gateway to feature articles, discussion boards, chats, and other valuable information on birds, cats, dogs, fish, horses, reptiles, and small pets.

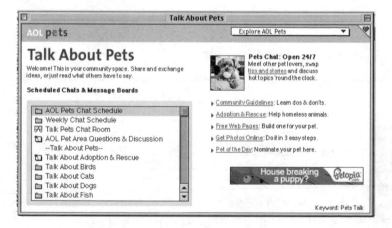

To chat with other pet lovers, select Talk About Pets from the main Pets area or type Keyword: **Pets Talk**. Here you'll find message boards and 24-hours chat rooms.

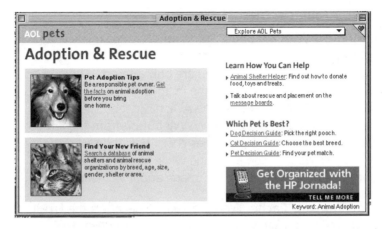

To access AOL's Adoption & Rescue area, select it from the main Pets area or type Keyword: **Animal Adoption**.

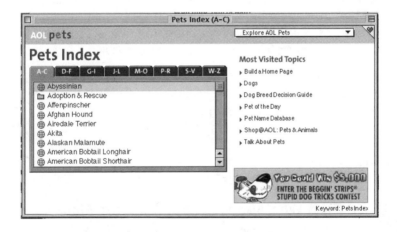

To learn about different breeds of pets on AOL, select Pets Index from the main Pets area or type Keyword: **Pets Index**.

MORE AMERICA ONLINE TIPS

Turning off Web graphics. Some sites have so many images that, depending on your connection speed, you can wait a long time for the page to load. If you are only interested in reading the information, you can turn the images off. To do this, head over to the **My AOL** icon on the AOL navigation toolbar and select **Preferences**. Select the **WWW** button from the left column. Uncheck the **Show Images** check box and click **OK**. Should you want to see an image while at a Web site, simply double-click on the box for the image and it will load.

Emptying your Cache. Web browser cache stores the HTML and graphics of a site you visited on your hard drive. This speeds things up when returning to a site while you're still logged on. However, when the cache fills up, performance can slow down. To empty your AOL's browser cache, go to the **My AOL** icon on the AOL navigation toolbar and select **Preferences**. Select the **WWW** button from the left column. Click the **Empty Cache Now** button, and click **OK**.

Using a Different Browser. Most people prefer to use Netscape Navigator or Internet Explorer to view Web pages instead of AOL's browser. Using a different browser while in AOL is simple: Once connected to AOL, minimize the AOL window (Mac users can close the window) and launch your favorite.

ISP Users Who Also Want AOL Can Save Money.

If you want an ISP and AOL, or if you have ISP access through work, school, or a high-speed Internet connection and want an AOL account too, sign up for AOL's Bring Your Own Access (BYOA) plan. It allows you unlimited connection through your ISP for $9.95 per month instead of AOL's usual $21.95 per month. If you currently have an AOL account and want to change to BYOA, type keyword **Billing** and follow the instructions. Note that if you have BYOA and sign on to AOL as a guest from someone else's AOL access number account, you will incur a ten-cents-per-minute surcharge.

HOW TO SHOP FOR OTHER INTERNET SERVICE PROVIDERS

If you don't want to use America Online, or if you used it and want to move on for whatever reason, it's time to look for an ISP. Currently there are thousands to select from, and it often becomes a daunting task to find the right ISP for your needs. Ask friends, co-workers, or neighbors for their recommendations. Find out why certain providers are liked or disliked. Check these additional guidelines:

- Look for an ISP with a fast connection (T1 or better, directly into the Internet's network backbone) and 56K bps connections that support the same connection standards as your modem.
- Inquire about technical support. Your ISP should help configure your browser (or provide you with software that will configure it for you) and be available around the clock to answer any questions you may have.
- Find out how long the company has been in business (four years or more is good), and how many customers it has (organizations in addition to individuals is a good sign). If it's a local provider, ask for customer references and call to find out what they like and dislike about their service.
- Monthly fees should be about $20 per month, and include unlimited connection time, 56K bps connections, free Web page hosting, and free e-mail.

Favorite National Internet Service Providers include **Earthlink** (**http://www.earthlink.net**), and **AT&T WorldNet** (**http://www.att.net**). For help in locating an ISP for your needs and budget, visit **The Lists** (**http://www.thelist.com**).

HIGH SPEED INTERNET ACCESS THROUGH CABLE AND DSL

There was a time when only certain businesses or those with megabucks were able to obtain high-speed Internet access. For the rest of us, the keyword was wait. Wait for the service to dial-up and connect. Wait for e-mail messages to appear. Wait for a Web page to load. And downloads? That was anything from a watch-a-sitcom wait to a watch-a-movie wait. Today, fast home Internet access that won't break the bank is increasing as cable and digital subscription line modems (DSL) are being offered in many—alas, not all—areas of the country. Both services are digital, not analog. That means there are no annoying dial-up sounds, and the service is always connected twenty-four hours a day, seven days a week. You need only launch your browser to be online.

Cable. The same two-way cable that brings cable television into your house can also handle high-speed data connections. The best way to find out whether cable Internet is available in your area is to call your local cable company. Some communities have only one-way cable for signals to come into your home. If you live in such a community, you'll have to wait for your cable company to first upgrade to coaxial (two-way cable) before Internet access is available.

If your cable company offers an Internet connection, ask if there are any special deals. When I had cable installed years ago, my installation was free because the company was running a promotion. Otherwise, expect to pay about $150–200 for installation—and make sure you thoroughly test drive your connection before allowing the technician to leave your house. Monthly fees are about $40–50, depending on whether you also have cable television from the same provider.

When I first subscribed to cable Internet, I had an incredibly fast connection since the service was new and not many subscribed. As cable Internet became popular in my town, my connection speed s-l-o-w-e-d, especially during peak hours of use. Why? Because a cable Internet connection is similar to a party telephone line (remember those?). It's a shared line. More people meant more congestion and slower rates of data flow. There were times when I considered making up stories of a hacker breaking into cable accounts just to scare my neighbors into canceling their service. Instead I kept calling the cable company to complain. The company either tired of my threats or received enough complaints that they made adjustments, as things are speedy again. How speedy? I recently downloaded the latest version of American Online in 4 minutes. The estimated download time for a 56k bps modem is 28 minutes; 28K bps: 56 minutes; and 14.4K bps: 1 hour and 52 minutes.

DSL. Also referred to as a digital subscription line, DSL allows fast Internet connections to homeowners (and small businesses) over a telephone line. Amazingly, it does not interfere with a normal telephone call. You can talk on the phone at the same time you sift through Web sites.

To find out if DSL is available in your area, call your local telephone company. It will determine where its nearest digital center is, if you reside within three miles of it, and whether your phone lines can handle the data flow. If you pass those tests, consider your keyword lucky. If you choose to proceed, some companies provide free installation while others charge anywhere from $150 to $350 (again, check for promotions). Monthly fees for average home users can range $40-70 per month (small business plans are higher). While the cost is generally higher than cable, DSL has a clear advantage—a dedicated line. The line is only yours, meaning a steady and predictable rate of speed starting at about ten-times faster than a 56K bps connection.

For more information on cable and DSL Internet access, see **Cable Modem Info** (**http://www.cablemodeminfo.com**), **Cable Modem Help** (**http://www.cablemodemhelp.com**), **Cable Modem Network** (**http://www.cable-modem.net**), **DSL Forum** (**http://www.adsl.com**), and **Everything DSL** (**http://www.everythingdsl.com**) which includes warnings about free DSL scams. Internet cable or DSL users running Windows 98/NT should visit **Speed Tweaks** (**http://www.cable-modems.org/articles/speed_tweaks**) to learn how to fine tune your Windows registry to improve your connection speed.

 SATELLITE CABLE ACCESS

While not as fast as cable or DSL, connecting to a satellite Internet service can be up to eight times faster than a 56K bps modem connection. For starters, you need a Pentium PC with Windows 95 or better, a 28.8K bps (or faster) modem, 32 MB of RAM, and 100 MB of hard disk space. Next you need to install a receiver dish antenna (cost about $200 to $400) and you must have a direct unobstructed line-of-sight to the satellite. Although you can align the dish yourself, it's probably worth the additional couple hundred dollars to pay someone who knows what they are doing. Unfortunately, even after everything is up and running smoothly, bad weather can knock the dish out-of-kilter which requires a service call. In areas where cable and DSL are not available, a satellite service is an option to Windows users wanting a faster connection. Different pricing plans range from $19.95 to $129.95 per month, without ISP. For more information, see **Hughes Network System's DirecPC** (**http://www.direcpc.com**), the country's leading satellite Internet service provider.

WHAT PET LOVERS NEED TO KNOW ABOUT BROWSERS

No matter what Internet service you use, in order to view the Web you need a browser. Years ago you also needed separate programs for doing other things on the Internet, such sending and retrieving e-mail, participating in Usenet newsgroups, or downloading files. Today's browsers have simplified things by including those features. The two most popular browsers are Netscape Navigator (or Communicator, a larger suite of programs with Navigator being the browser) and Microsoft's Internet Explorer. Both are free.

While your ISP will supply you with a browser, chances are you already have one or both installed in your hard drive. You do not have to use the browser that came with your computer. You can use whatever you wish, including text-only browsers or other browsers such as AOL's, and many people regularly alternate between a couple.

Configuring your browser can be tricky. Make sure your ISP helps set up your browser or provides you with software that will configure it for you. Once configured, copy these settings (located in the TCP/IP control panel) and keep them in a safe place.

How and Why You Should Keep Your Browser Current

Most people are happy using a particular program because it's easier than having to upgrade. However, it's important that you keep your browser up-to-date. Besides keeping your browser compatible with the latest developments in Internet technology, using the latest version also keeps your computer secure by fixing whatever security holes might need to be patched.

You can find out what version of Netscape you have by pulling down the Help menu and selecting **About Navigator** (or **About Communicator**, depending on what's installed). Upgrade if it's less than version 4.7. Click the **Netscape** icon in the Navigation Toolbar (if you don't see it, select **View/Show/Navigation Toolbar** from the menu) or head over to **Netscape** (**http://www.netscape.com**) and select **download**. A smart-download feature is available that may help speed up your download process.

Click the Netscape icon in the Navigation Toolbar to go directly to Netscape's Web page. From there, click download.

You can learn what version of Internet Explorer you have by pulling down the Help menu and selecting **About Internet Explorer**. If it's less than version 5.0, upgrade. Click the **IE** icon on the far right of the button bar to go to Microsoft's IE download page (if you don't see it, select **View/Button Bar** from the menu). Windows users can access the page by typing **<http://www.microsoft.com/windows/ie/download>** and Macintosh users can access the page by typing **<http://www.microsoft.com/mac/products/ie>**.

Click the Internet Explorer icon on the far right of the button bar to go directly to Microsoft's IE download page.

Web Access for Older Computers

To get some sort of Internet access, you don't need a new computer. Even those with an original Apple II, circa 1979, can tap in. To be able to view graphics, however, you'll need a computer manufactured within the last eight years.

Opera (**http://www.opera.com**) is an inexpensive browser that includes news and e-mail. In addition to being a browser alternative to the big two, it works without hitch on a 486 PC with 8 MB of RAM and Windows 3.1—and it can work on older systems too. A Mac version of Opera may be available by the time you read this.

If you're running an older Macintosh (even a black/white Mac), head to **Chris Adam's Web Browser for Antique Macs** Web page (**http://www.edprint.demon.co.uk/se/macweb.html**). Chris offers an informative page detailing which browser is best to use with your Mac and includes downloads for Tradewave's MacWeb, NCSA Mosaic, early versions of Netscape, and others.

HOW TO ACCESS A WEB PAGE

Now that your browser is up and running, it's time to surf the Web.

Address: @ http://www.petsmart.com/

To access a Web page, type the Web site's address (commonly called **URL** or "Uniform Resource Locator") into the white window bar—called **Location** in Netscape or **Address** in IE—and press **Enter** (**Return** on a Mac). For example, to access the PETsMART.com site, type <http://www.petsmart.com>.

Because each address is unique, it's extremely important that URLs are typed exactly as they appear. If you're missing a single letter, a punctuation mark, or using a lower-case letter instead of an upper case letter, the Web browser will not be able to locate the desired page.

You can cut and paste URLs from other documents into the location or address bar. Use your mouse to highlight the address. Then press **Ctrl-C** (**⌘-C** on a Mac) to copy the address. Use your mouse to click onto the location or address bar, highlight any current address in the box, and press **Ctrl-V** (**⌘-V** on a Mac) to paste in the new address. Then press **Enter** (**Return** on a Mac).

HOW TO NAVIGATE THE WEB WITHOUT GETTING LOST AND HOW TO FIND YOUR WEB PAGE HISTORY

When viewing Web pages, you'll notice certain words are underlined and in a color, usually different from the rest of the text. These words are known as **hyperlinks**, links, or hotlinks. By clicking on a link, you are transported to a new Web site—either a new page on the site you're visiting or an entirely different site. You can easily jump from Web site to Web site (also called "surfing the Web") by clicking on links. Often images are links to other sites, too. With so much jumping from site to site, you may find yourself lost and wanting to get back to some earlier sites you visited. Here's how:

Click the **Back** button on the Navigation or Button bar to return to the previously visited Web site (or **Go/Back** from the menu).

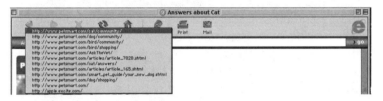

Right-click (click-hold on a Mac) on the **Back** button to display a drop-down list of Web sites you recently visited. To return to a site, simply select it. (Selecting Go from the menu will display a similar drop-down menu.)

On Internet Explorer, selecting **GO** from the menu will also display a day-by-day history of the sites you visited (or you can select **Window/History** from the menu bar). To change the number of sites saved or to clear the history, select **Edit/Preferences** from the menu. A dialog box will appear. Select **Web Browser** in the left column, and select **Advanced**. In the History portion of the dialog box, edit the **Places Visited** box or click the **Clear History** button.

To display **History** information in Netscape Navigator, select **Communicator/Tools/History** from the menu. To change how long Web pages are tracked in the History window or to clear the History, select **Edit/Preferences** from the menu. A dialog box will appear. Select Navigator from the left column. Type in the number of days in the box or click the **Expire Now** button to clear the history. Note that on the Mac OS, page visits are only recorded for the current session and will expire when you quit the application.

T I P

A URL (Uniform Resource Locator) is the unique address that takes you to a specific Internet site. The first couple letters in the address (called the URL prefix) indicate what type of Internet site you're connecting to. The most common prefix is **http**, which stands for "hyper-text transfer protocol." Other protocols include **ftp**, which stands for "file transfer protocol" and is used for transferring files; **news**, for connecting to a newsgroup; and **mailto**, for displaying an outgoing e-mail window. The URL prefix is always followed by a colon and two slashes :*//*. This punctuation separates the prefix from the document's address. The most common URL addresses are to sites located on the World Wide Web. They start **http://www**. Following the **www** is a period, referred to as **dot**, and used to separate different sections of the Web address. Next comes the domain name, the entity that runs the Web site, another dot, and a three-letter suffix indicating the type of entity that runs the site. Common suffixes include **.com** (commercial), **.edu** (university), **.org** (nonprofit organization), and **.gov** (government). For example, <**http://www.petsmart.com**> is a commercial site on the Wide World Web.

The pages (or documents) that make up a Web site are stored either on the domain name site or in directories or subdirectories of the site (depending on the site's organization—and similar to the directory path on your computer). Each slash of a URL represents a directory. The more slashes, the more subdirectories. The document name of a particular page is located after the last slash and generally ends with **.html** or **.htm**.

HOW TO SEARCH FOR WEB SITES

If you're trying to locate information, the Internet is the place to look. But with its seemingly gazillion pages of information and absolutely no type of centralized organization system (imagine an unalphabetized phone book), locating what you're looking for can be like finding the proverbial needle in a haystack. If you're faced with a "Not Found" error message for a site you seek, or if you're looking for more information, try an Internet search service. Here's an overview:

- **Directory.** Perfect for looking for general information on a particular topic, directory services employ people to view individual sites and classify worthy pages into subject category and subcategory schemes. Yahoo! (**http://www.yahoo.com**), LookSmart (**http://www.looksmart.com**), and InfoSpace (**http://www.infospace.com**) are three popular services.
- **Search Engine.** It's what to use when looking for specific information on a topic. Its index of sites is mainly created by "spiders" or "bots" (short for robots) that visit Web sites and add whatever pages it finds into a large database. AltaVista (**http://www.altavista.com**) and Lycos (**http://www.lycos.com**) are two search engines, both of which also include directories. Because search engines primarily rely on spiders rather than people to gather information, far more Web sites are indexed in search engines than are found on directories.
- **Metasearch Engine.** Use it to investigate multiple search sites with a single action. MetaCrawler (**http://www.meta crawler.com**), SavvySearch (**http://www.savvysearch.com**), and Dogpile (**http://www.dogpile.com**).

To use a search engine, enter a series of keywords in the designated window and click the "search" button. The engine will then search its database and present a list of links based on those keywords. It's not uncommon for a search to result in thousands of "hits" or "matches"—far too many to sort through. To get better search results, use quotation marks around keywords to search for exact phrases. Also, read the advanced search options at the search engine's site for additional advice on how you can narrow your search.

Ask Jeeves (**http://www.askjeeves.com**) is a different approach to a search engine. Instead of typing keywords, you type in a question and it presents sites that may answer.

How to Find a Web Site That Moved

Web site owners often update their sites on a regular basis. Sometimes in the process of updating, a site is overhauled with new directories and subdirectories. If this happens, the document you're looking for may have been moved or renamed and may not be in the place your URL points to. In this case, you will get a *Not Found* error message.

Try finding the page by deleting the last portion of the URL, working backwards to the slash. For example, PETsMART.com offers PETsMART Premier food at its site. The URL is<**http://www.petsmart.com/dog/ shopping/food_center/petsmart_premier/psearch.shtml**>. If you typed the URL and got a **Not Found** message, delete the "/psearch.shtml" portion of the URL and hit **Enter** (**Return** on a Mac). If there's nothing there or you get a strange error message, continue working back through the URL until you locate the page you're after or get to the domain name where hopefully you can search the site and find the desired page. For example, you can delete the last portion of the URL and go from:

http://www.petsmart.com/dog/shopping/food_center/ petsmart_premier/psearch.shtml

to

http://www.petsmart.com/dog/shopping/food_center/pets- mart_premier

to

http://www.petsmart.com/dog/shopping/food_center

to

http://www.petsmart.com/dog/shopping

to

http://www.petsmart.com/dog

to

http://www.petsmart.com

Sometimes when working back through the URL, you can arrive at a directory listing of files. If so, look for a file that ends with a .html or .htm and click on it. Both extensions indicate the file is a document (.gif and .jpg are image extensions). If you get an "Access Denied" message, try going further back through the URL.

 *Working back through a URL address can often help you to locate a page that has moved. But it is not insurance that the page still exists. Sometimes the site owner may move to a new domain. In that case, see How to Search for Web Sites in this chapter. Sometimes the site owner may delete a page or delete the entire site. In that case, it's gone.*

Sites starting with **http://** are so common that newer browsers don't require you to type that portion of the URL. For example, if you type <**www.petsmart.com**> into your location or address window, your browser will automatically insert **http://** and whisk you to the PETsMART.com site.

How to Find a Picture that You Saved on Your Hard Drive.

You know you downloaded a graphic, but you can't find it. If you can't remember the name of the graphic that you saved, go back to the Web page and click on it again to see the name. Then, if you have a PC running Windows 95 or higher, click **Start**, then **Find**, and finally type the name of the file. Windows will find it for you. If you're using a Mac, select **Sherlock** (or **Find File** on an older system) from the Apple menu. Type in the file name, and Sherlock will find it for you.

Does Your Connection Seem SLOW?

- If your connection seems slow, check that your modem speed is properly set. If your software is set at a speed that's faster than your modem is capable of handling, performance will slow down. If you're not sure what it should be set at, experiment by lowering the speed and testing to see if you get better performance. If you have no idea what your modem speed should be set to at or how to reset it, call your ISP for help. If you have a cable Internet connection, call your provider and ask that a signal be sent to your modem to confirm that it's properly set.
- If you upgraded your browser and things seem slow, check the browser's minimum requirements. It's possible your computer may need more physical memory.
- The biggest reason for your connection speed to slow is heavy traffic. Like hitting a crowded toll booth when coming off a highway, if there are too many people on the Internet or too many trying to access the same site at the same time, things slow down. Peak traffic times are often late afternoon and early evening. Unfortunately, like real traffic, there's no way to avoid traffic unless you avoid rush hour.

Use Third-Party Software to Organize Your Bookmarks. If you love hordes of bookmarks and want to use them while in different browsers, consider a low-cost bookmark utility program. Such programs allow you to save and organize your bookmarks in a central location accessible by any browser. A good place to download them is from **C/net's Shareware.Com** (**http://www.shareware.com**). Search for the phrase "bookmark organizer." For PCs, try the $29 shareware program LinkMan Professional from Thomas Reimann. For Macs, try **URL Manager Pro**, the $25 shareware program from Alco Blom (**http://www.url-manager.com**).

HOW TO CREATE AND ORGANIZE BOOKMARKS

Web browsers let you "bookmark" sites. A bookmark allows your browser to revisit a selected site with a mouse-click rather than you having to retype the site's URL. Bookmarks are easy to create and use, and it's not difficult to amass a large quantity of bookmarks in a short period of time. Fortunately, browsers also allow you to organize and customize your bookmarks.

• How to Add and Use a Bookmark

To add a bookmark in Navigator while you are viewing a site, click **Bookmarks** (Mac users select **Bookmarks/Add** from the menu). To add a bookmark to Explorer while you are viewing a site, select **Favorites/Add to Favorites** from the menu. Note that Explorer calls bookmarks "Favorites." You'll notice that both Navigator and Explorer come preloaded with a selection of bookmarks to sites they believe you'll enjoy visiting. To use a bookmark, simply click **Bookmark** or **Favorites** on the menu and select the site you want to visit.

To add a bookmark to Explorer while you are viewing a site, select Favorite/Add to Favorites from the menu.

To use a bookmark in Explorer, click Favorites on the menu and select the site you want to visit.

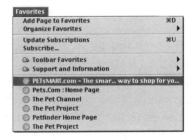

• How to Organize and Edit Bookmarks

To organize your bookmarks in Navigator, click the **Bookmarks** icon and select **Edit Bookmarks** (Mac users select **Bookmarks/Edit Bookmarks** from the menu). A dialog box appears with a list of your bookmarks. Click the item above where you put to place a new folder or a new dividing line. To add a folder, select

File/New Folder from the menu; type a name for the folder and click OK. To add a separator, or dividing line, select **File/New Separator**. To edit bookmarks click the **Bookmarks** icon and select **Edit Bookmarks** (Mac users select **Bookmarks/Edit Bookmarks** from the menu. You can drag folders to reorder them, and delete folders or sites. To delete a folder or site, click to select it, then hit the delete key or select **Edit/Clear** from the menu.

To organize your bookmarks in Explorer, select **View/ Explorer Bar** from the menu. Click the **Favorites** tab. Click the **Organize** button to create as many new named folders or dividers as you need. (You can also select **Favorites/Organize Favorites/New Folder** and **Favorites/Organize/New Divider** from the menu.) Then drag the link icon of a site to move its link into a folder. You can drag and arrange folders and dividers to suit your needs. If you want to change the name of a folder, click its name to highlight it (sometimes you need to first click outside the lower right and drag across towards the upper left to get the name highlighted), type in a new name, and press **Enter** (or **Return**). To delete a site, select it in a similar manner and press the **Delete** button. If the Explorer bar is open, you can also add the URL of a site that you are currently visiting by clicking the **Add** button.

• How to Create an Internet Shortcut by Adding Sites to Your Windows or Macintosh Desktop

If you have a favorite site that you visit daily, you can add a shortcut to it from your Windows 95 (or higher) or Mac desktop. If the page you want to add a shortcut to is loaded in Netscape, use your mouse to drag the bookmark icon (to the left of the URL location window) from the browser to your desktop (in Navigator, drag the icon located to the left of the URL). A shortcut icon will appear. By clicking the icon, your browser will launch, your ISP will connect, and you'll be whisked to the Web site. Another way to add a shortcut is selecting a site from your list of bookmarks and dragging its icon to your desktop. In Navigator, select **Bookmarks/Edit Bookmarks**. In Explorer, select **View/Explorer Bar** and click the **Favorites** tab.

HOW TO PRINT AND SAVE WEB PAGES AND IMAGES

• To Save a Web Page

After the page is fully loaded, select **File/Save As** from the menu. A dialog box will appear. Name the file and save it as either **text**, which you can open through a word processing program, or **source** which creates an HTML (the language that a Web page is written in) document you can read through your browser while offline.

A source document will include formatted text and placement holders for images, but it will not include the actual images unless you download each and place them in the same directory (or file) as you saved the source (HTML) document. See below for how to download an image.

• To Print a Web Page

After the page has fully loaded, select **File/Print** from the menu. If the page has frames, first click in the frame you want to print (I often select some of the text to make sure the frame is selected). Then select **File/Print Frame** from the menu.

• To Save an Image From a Web Page to Your Hard Drive

Position your mouse cursor over the image. Right-click on the image (click-hold on a Mac). A pop-up menu will appear. Select **Save Image As** or **Save Picture As**. You can later view it in your browser or in a graphics program.

✋ *You can save and print Web pages and images, but you should only do so for your personal use. When Web site owners graciously publish their Web sites for all the world to enjoy, that doesn't mean you can take information from the site and use it however you please. If you want to use something for any other purpose than personal use, write the Web site owner and get permission. Anything else—including any type of distribution or adding an image or copied text to your own Web site—is a violation of copyright law. Don't do it! For more information, see* **The Copyright Website** *(***http://www.benedict.com***) and the U.S.Copyright Office (***http://lcweb.loc.gov/copyright***).*

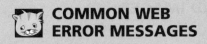

COMMON WEB ERROR MESSAGES

✋ 400 Bad Request

The requested URL could not be retrieved.

Reason: Your browser could not find the requested site.

Fix: The culprit of this common error message is a typo in the URL (I do this all the time). Check that the URL is typed correctly, including all punctuation and upper and lower case letters. If you continue to get the message, there's a good chance the site no longer exists.

✋ 404 Not Found

The requested URL was not found on this server.

Reason: Your browser found the service on which the Web site was or is hosted, but it cannot find the particular page you are looking for.

Fix: Try working back through the URL as explained earlier in this chapter to see if you can locate the Web site. Also check the suffix of the document. If it ends in ".htm" try ".html" and vice versa.

✋ 503 Service Unavailable

Reason: Something isn't working somewhere—either the ISP is down or your system isn't working.

Fix: Make sure your telephone wire is firmly connected in the jack. If you have an external modem, check the back to make sure the telephone wire is secure. If the problem persists, call your ISP.

✋ DNS Lookup Failure
or The Server Does Not Have a DNS Entry.

Reason: This common error means that the Domain Name System (the way domain names are translated into unique Internet addresses or IP numbers) could not translate the URL to a working Internet address.

Fix: Often this can be fixed by clicking on the **Reload** button. Also check the spelling of the domain name to confirm it's correct. Otherwise, try the URL later in the day. If you continue to get the message, it's probable that the domain name no longer exists.

✋ No Response from Server
or Server Is Busy

Reason: In the first instance, your browser is unable to get a response from the Web site's host computer, most likely due to heavy traffic. In the second, it's a common error message issued when too many people are trying to access a popular site.

Fix: In either case, try the URL in a short time or at the end of the day, and click the Reload button.

T I P

Mac Users Try John Moe's **Net Print** (**http://www93.pair.com/johnmoe**). This $10 shareware program allows you to highlight any text in your browser window (and other programs, too) and print or save it.

GENERAL
WEB SAFETY TIPS

• **Never give anyone your online password(s),** credit card numbers, social security number, or mother's maiden name. Unfortunately, unscrupulous individuals can obtain your ISP username and e-mail you under the guise of being an AOL, Earthlink, or other ISP employee seeking information to verify your account. Don't ever believe it, and do not respond. Instead, report such letters to your ISP.

• **When selecting a password, don't use anything obvious**—like your date of birth. Instead, use your imagination, and create combinations of words and numbers. Periodically change your password. If a site requires you to create an identification name and password, make it different from the username and password you use to access the Web.

• **Don't let your browser remember your passwords for you.** Instead, keep a separate record of usernames and passwords in a text file or in a Rolodex or other filing system away from your computer.

• **Do not answer any type of junk mail,** especially ones that say "respond to this letter to be removed from our list." Often a response indicates to the sender that it reached a valid user, and it may result in more junk mail. Never forward a chain letter or virus warning. Most are a hoax. Visit **Urban Legends Archive** (**http://www.urbanlegends.com**) and Vmyths (**http://www.Vmyths.com**) for information on chain letters and hoaxes. If you fear a genuine computer virus, check the **CERT Computer Virus Resource Center** (**http://www.cert.org/ other_sources/viruses.html**) which includes extensive resources on computer viruses, including the latest virus-related news.

• **Never click on hyperlinks within an e-mail message sent to you by a stranger.** Such a site can whisk you to a official-looking Web site which claims one thing while the site is instead downloading a virus to your computer.

• **Never open a file attachment from someone you don't know.** It is the single best way to avoid contracting a computer virus.

• **Supervise your children while on the Net** by talking to them regularly about what they're doing online and by being involved with their online adventures. Warn them often not to meet strangers in person they may meet online, even if they insist the new friend is a teenager—sometimes they are not.

WEB SHOPPING SAFETY TIPS

• Currently there are over 3,500 businesses on the Web that offer the **Better Business Bureau's BBBOnline** seal of approval (**http://www.bbbonline.com**). To obtain the seal, businesses must (among other things) provide security, friendly dispute resolution, and stand behind its advertised claims. If you see the seal  on a site, click it. It should bring you to the BBB Online and provide details of the store. If you only see the seal or want to learn if a retail site is a participant, search the **BBB Online** (**http://www.bbbonline.org/database/search/default.cfm**).

• Read a site's privacy policy to understand what personal information will be requested and why and how it will be used. You can usually find a link to the site's privacy policy or by checking the site's legal terms. If you cannot find a privacy policy, e-mail the site and ask for it. If the site doesn't respond or doesn't have one, do business elsewhere.

• Some sites carry the TRUSTe seal.  The seal is only awarded to sites that maintain established privacy principles. Clicking on the seal should bring you to the site's privacy policy. It should not bring you to the **TRUSTe** Web site (**http://www.truste.org**). If it does, be suspicious and search to see if the retail site is a participating member (**http://www.truste.org/users/users_lookup.html**).

How to Tell if a Web Site is Secure and How to Turn on Your Browser Security Features

A secure Web site uses a form of sophisticated encryption that scrambles your transmitted information and keeps it safe from prying eyes. Your browser has features to alert you when you are entering and leaving a secure site and when you are sending information to an unencrypted site.

To open the security preferences in Netscape Navigator, click on the **padlock** icon in the lower left corner of the browser window. Select Navigator in the left column, check the show warning boxes, and click **OK**. To open the security preferences in Internet Explorer, select **Edit/Preferences** from the menu. Then select **Web Broswer/Security** from the left column in the dialog box. Check the security alert boxes and click **OK**.

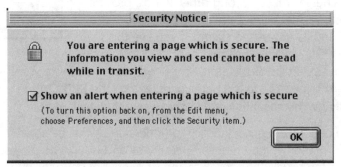

When entering a secure page, an dialog box will appear alert you that the page is secure.

When at a secure site, you'll see an "s" after the <**http**> portion of the URL. An unsecured site will read <**http**>; a secure site will read <**https**>. For example: **https://www.buysafe.com/purchase**.

On a secure site you will see a unbroken key or a closed padlock on the bottom of your browser window.

- When considering a site to shop from, make sure you understand its return policies. Retail sites often offer different delivery methods at various costs. Be sure to designate your preference.

- Never give your credit card details within an e-mail message. E-mail is not secure.

- Never submit your credit card information or bank account information to an unsecured site. An unsecured site means the information in it can be intercepted.

- When shopping on the Web, always use a credit card. If you have any problem, you can contact the credit company and either get the matter resolved or possibly get a refund. If for any reason, however, you are uncomfortable using a credit card, ask the site's customer support if an alternate form of payment can be made (check, money order, COD).

- Always keep a written record of each Internet transaction, including the seller's name, address, telephone number, any e-mail messages, and a description of what you ordered, price, and terms. Be sure to compare it to the charge on your credit card bill.

TIP

Want to become a smarter online shopper? Visit **Safe Shopping.org** (**http://www.safeshopping.org**) from the American Bar Association and **The Better Business Bureau** (**http://www.bbb.org**) for a wonderful selection of articles. If you have a problem or suspect fraud, visit the **National Fraud Information Center** (**http://www.fraud.org**) and the **Internet Fraud Complaint Center** (**http://www.ifccfbi.gov**) for help.

free Big Web Sites for Pet Lovers

There is a menagerie of pets in this world and hordes of marvelous Web sites devoted to them.

This chapter features the content-rich prodigious sites, the ones you'll want to bookmark and return to again and again. On them you can read the latest news, learn how best to care and understand your pet, and chitchat with other lovers of furry, feathered, or scaled creatures. These sites are portals to the world of dogs, cats, fish, birds, small animals, and reptiles—and a great place to start your cyber-adventure.

 PETSMART
http://www.petsmart.com

This treasure includes expert-compiled descriptive information for over 500 different breeds and species. Countless articles are available about pet health, behavior, nutrition, training, and other topics. Ask the Vet includes weekly vet questions and answers and a considerable selection of articles—such as camping with your pet, removing a fish hook from your pet, and what to do if your pet gets skunked. You can sign up for three different newsletters, share your pet pictures and stories, enter contests, post questions and answers, and chat with other pet lovers. Looking for a PETsMART store? Use the Store Locator to find one near you.

For free dog and cat product samples from the Harts Groups, visit **Pet Talk America's Free Stuff** page (**http://www.pettalk.com/free.html**).

NETPETS
http://www.netpets.org

NetPets is a nonprofit organization whose compelling goal is to be all things to all pet and animal-oriented persons.

IVILLAGE PETS
http://www.ivillage.com/pets

Get the lowdown on taking care of your pets from iVillage Pets. Tools include a breed selector, pet name finder, pet homepages, and resources. Click the Experts link for dog-training advice and holistic vet care. A free Pet Gazette newsletter is available.

MY PET STOP.COM
http://www.mypetstop.com

This world of pet information includes sections on dog, cats, birds, and fish with nutrition, ownership, health care, behavior, and travel/moving advice. The Breed Stop details information on different breeds and connects you to a breeders discussion group. Use the search engine in Vet Stop to search articles and FAQS for health and behavior advice, or tap into the Vet Locator for a directory of over 2,900 hospitals accredited by the American Animal Hospital Association.

MSN PETS & ANIMALS
http://pets.msn.com

*The latest animal news and pet care fill this lively site. Animal cams allow you to view live images of crocodiles, horses, lions, various pets, and sharks. If you have children, be sure to visit **Kidz Pets & Animals** (**http://kids.msn.com;kidz/petsanimals.asp**) for educational articles, a polar bear cam, and other fun.*

Looking for even more pet-related sites?

Tap into these sites:

Pet Directory (**http://www.petdir.com**)
AllCritters (**http://www.allcritters.com**)
AnyPet.com (**http://anypet.com**)
The Petwork (**http://www.petwork.com**)
The Electronic Zoo (**http://netvet.wustl.edu/e-zoo.htm**)
The Tame Beast (**http://www.tamebeast.com**).

ALL PETS.COM
http://www.allpets.com

Ever wonder how a dog's teeth are cleaned? Head to Pet Flicks to view a fascinating teeth-cleaning procedure. You can also view online videos for senior dog and cat care, selecting a puppy or kitten, pet grooming, surgical procedures, and other topics. The Petcyclopedia contains vast pet guidance. If you have a question, visit the Community section for answers.

THE PET CHANNEL
http://www.thepetchannel.com

The Pet Channel offers plenty of news, articles and expert advice in health, training and other pet-related topics. Be sure to visit Fun Stuff for laughs, a kids' corner, and a pet gallery.

PETCO
http://www.petco.com

Visit Petco Tips for a collection of informational tips—including topics on pets, products, and pet care. PetPourri includes pet photos, stories, and coloring pages for kids of all ages. Tap into Locate a Petco to find a store in your area.

ANIMAL NEWS
http://www.animalnews.com

Aiming to reflect the broad spectrum of issues and interests involving people and their pets, this site features headline news; forums to discuss animal issues, dogs, cats, birds, wildlife, marine life, rescue, and adoptions; ask the vet questions and answers; free newsletters, and resources.

Need a name for your new pet? Head to **Bow Wow Meow—Pet Names with Personality** (**http://www.bowwow.com.au**) for thousands of names, their meanings, and their popularity rating. The **Worldwide Pet Names Project** (**http://www.wellwell well.com/petnames/all.html**) boasts over 7,400 pet names.

*To find a Hawaiian name for your pet, tap into Hawaiian Pet Names (**http://www.hisurf.com/hawaiian/petnames.html**).*

© 2000 Adtrix Internet Group, LLC

PETOPIA— PETCO'S INTERNET PET PARADISE
http://www.petopia.com

You'll find an extensive library of over 1,500 articles covering everything from first vet visits to healthy old age. Additionally, columnists celebrate the humorous and touching aspects of living with pets, and leading authorities offer valuable advice on pet care and behavior issues. Chats and several lively message boards are also available.

THE PET PROJECT
http://www.thepetproject.com

Visit the House of News to keep up-to-date on pet happenings. Sign up for a free newsletter, ask the experts your question, listen to pet-related audio streams, or join in other pet-related fun.

YAHOO! PETS
http://pets.yahoo.com

Includes articles, pet chats, message boards, and a plethora of related links.

FREE WEB SITES OF MAGAZINES FOR PET LOVERS

MENAGERIE— THE MAGAZINE FOR PETS AND THEIR PEOPLE
http://www.menagerie.on.ca

PET LIFE WEB
http://www.petlifeweb.com

ANIMAL NETWORK—FANCY PUBLICATIONS
http://www.animalnetwork.com

ANIMAL SHELTERING MAGAZINE
http://www.animalsheltering.org/programs/companion/
animal_sheltering/index.html

PET VIEW MAGAZINE ONLINE
http://www.petview.com/index.html

IT'S ABOUT ANIMALS NEWSPAPER COLUMNS FROM BOB DEFRANCO
http://www.canines.com/library/aboutanimals

ARK ONLINE—THE MAGAZINE FOR PEOPLE WHO CARE ABOUT ANIMALS
http://www.arkonline.com

SIMPLY PETS PETNEWS
http://www.simplypets.com/news

DR. SPIEGEL'S NEWSPAPER COLUMNS OF FASCINATING PET STORIES
http://www.petpsych.com/news.htm

ALL PETS.COM MAGAZINE
http://www.allpets.com/magazine

BEST FRIENDS
http://www.bestfriends.org/news/newshome.htm

Did you know that seniors who own dogs go to the doctor less than those who do not? Or that pets decrease the feeling of loneliness and isolation in their owners? Head to the **Health Benefits of Having A Pet** (**http://deltasociety.org/dsc000.htm**) where The Delta Society, the leading international resource for the human-animal bond, trumpets the health benefits of pet ownership.

Want to let the world know how special your pet is? Nominate it for **Pet of the Day** (**http://www.petoftheday.com**).

CHAPTER 3

free Web Hangouts for Pet Lovers

Who will share your joy when Tweetie finally whistles a rousing rendition of "Here Comes the Sun?" And who will want to hear every detail of Muffy's latest antics? And when you have questions about a new biscuit recipe for Fido, who can provide fast answers? Other pet lovers, of course! And often the best place to find pet lovers eager to share lively stories and advice is through the Internet. Joining a discussion group, or forum—bulletin boards, chat rooms, newsgroups, mailing lists—gives you the ability to communicate with people from all over the world who share your passion for pets. No matter what time of day or night, someone, somewhere, is out there ready to provide whole-hearted inspiration, encouragement, and solutions.

Throughout this book, you'll see sites with a chat icon indicating that you can find other pet lovers to converse with through some type of discussion group or forum on the Web site. This chapter will help you understand how they work and how to locate more.

The different types of forums include:

• **Newsgroups.** Newsgroups are unmoderated public discussion forums, also called Usenet (for Users Network), on which you can post and reply to messages from other users in a bulletin board fashion. Newsgroups are divided into major categories, called hierarchies—such as *rec* for recreation, *soc* for society and culture, and *biz* for business. Each hierarchy is followed by a period and a subcategory. For example, rec can include rec.pet. There are thousands of subcategories, often containing further subcategories such as rec.pet.birds. To locate newsgroups, see the sites in this chapter.

In the past to participate in a newsgroup, you needed to install a newsreader (for example **News Rover** available for free at **http://www.newsrover.com**). Today the easiest way to participate in a newsgroup is to use **Deja.com Usenet Discussion**

Service (**http://www.deja.com/usenet**) where you tap into messages directly from the Web. Additionally, your Web browser or AOL's software can be configured to "subscribe" to newsgroups. See your browser's online help or use AOL keyword **Help** for guidance.

Note that subscribing to a newsgroup can result in unwanted e-mail. For this reason, it's advisable that you first obtain a free e-mail account—such as **Excite Mail** (**http://www.mailexcite.com**) or Yahoo Mail (http://mail.yahoo.com)—and use this address rather than your primary e-mail address for your newsgroups.

✋ *Warning!* *While there are many informative Usenet newsgroups devoted to pet enthusiasts, they are unmoderated and uncensored. This means anything goes, including pornographic references.*

• **Chat.** A chat is a form of Internet communication that allows two or more people to have a real-time conversation. As you type and send your message, it is immediately relayed to those who are logged onto their computer and participating in the chat. A chat can take place on a Web page that supports a chat room or on an IRC channel. IRC stands for Internet Relay Chat, and it requires special software to participate. The software is generally free, and information on obtaining and configuring it is available from the Web site hosting the IRC chat.

• **E-Mail List.** An e-mail list is a forum in which participants subscribe to and receive messages by e-mail. More detailed information is included in this chapter.

• **Bulletin Board.** Bulletin Boards (or message boards) are generally located on large Web sites. You select a particular topic and can read posted text messages. You can also reply to messages—either publicly or privately.

NETIQUETTE

When posting to any Internet forum, it's important to know your netiquette—the rules of online etiquette. Here are some tips:

• Never send a file attachment (such as a picture of your pooch). Many servers cannot handle attachments.

• NEVER USE ALL CAPITALS in your message. It's hard to read and perceived as shouting.

• Never include personal information such as your address or phone number in a public list. Many lists are archived, meaning they are accessible long after you send it.

• Never forward warnings of computer viruses, pitches for donations, or other chain letters. Almost always these letters are a hoax, and your well-meaning intention could result in you being blasted with angry e-mail, in addition to further circulating the hoax. See General Web Safety Tips in Chapter 1 for more information.

• Use a descriptive title in your subject line so your readers will know what your message is about.

• Send your message as text only, not as text and HTML (see your browser's preferences to correct).

• If a list pertains to a specific topic, keep your posts to that topic. If off-topic messages are allowed, be sure to indicate that you are off topic (OT) in the subject line of your message.

• If you are replying to a particular message, copy the portion of the original message that you are responding to. Don't assume that everyone understands what you are replying to.

• Before sending your post, read it over carefully. Limit jokes and sarcasm, as they often do not translate well over an international audience. Remember that you message will linger for a long time in cyberspace.

• For more information on netiquette, visit **Dear Miss Emily Postnews** (**http://www.templetons.com/brad/emily.html**), a humorous look on proper Net behavior written by Brad Templeton.

Free Directories to Newsgroups, Mailing Lists, and Chats

DEJA.COM USENET DISCUSSION SERVICE
http://www.deja.com/usenet

You can read newsgroup postings directly through this Web site rather than through a traditional newsreader. Additionally, this site boasts the largest searchable archive of newsgroups and popular forums, too. To post to a newsgroup, you first need to register— but registration is free.

THE DIRECTORY OF PUBLICLY ACCESSIBLE MAILING LISTS
http://paml.net

Stephanie da Silva maintains this premier collection of mailing lists. An index and search engine are included.

T I P

There are many informative Usenet newsgroups devoted to pet enthusiasts. This list will get you started:

rec.pets	**rec.pets.herp**
rec.pets.dogs.misc	**rec.pets.birds**
rec.pets.dogs.activities	**rec.pets.parrots.misc**
rec.pets.dogs.behaviors	**rec.pets.parrots.african-grey**
rec.pets.dogs.breeds	**rec.pets.parrots.amazons**
rec.pets.dogs.health	**rec.pets.parrots.cockatiels**
rec.pets.dogs.info	**alt.pets.parrots.cockatiels**
rec.pets.dogs.rescue	**alt.pets.parrots.african-grey**
rec.pets.cats.announce	**alt.pets.birds.softbills**
rec.pets.cats.misc	**rec.aquaria.misc**
rec.pets.cats.health	**rec.aquaria.freshwater.plants**
rec.pets.cats.anecdotes	**rec.aquaria.tech**
rec.pets.cats.rescue	**rec.aquaria.freshwater.**
rec.pets.cats.community	**goldfish**
rec.pets.cats.announce	**rec.equestrian**
rec.pets.ferrets	

META-LIST
http://www.meta-list.net

Search over 200,000 e-mail list and newsletters.

LISZT—THE MAILING LIST DIRECTORY
http://www.liszt.com

Liszt features a searchable database of over 90,000 mailing lists. You can also find discussion groups, newsgroups, and IRC chats.

E-GROUPS
http://www.egroups.com

Start an e-mail group or find one at this site featuring a searchable database and groups

TILE NET
http://tile.net

FORUM ONE
http://www.forumone.com

Web Sites Offering Free Forums, Bulletin Boards, Mailing Lists, and Chats for Pet Lovers

FREE FORUMS AND BULLETIN BOARDS

YAHOO! PETS MESSAGE BOARDS
http://messages.yahoo.com/yahoo/Family___Home/Pets/index.html

Yahoo! Pets offers a variety of message boards for birds, cats, dogs, fish, and other pets.

PETOPIA COMMUNITY
http://www.petopia.com

Click the Community link to tap into active dog, cat, and other pet message boards. Transcripts of past chats are also available.

THE PET VINE
http://www.thepetvine.com

Have a question? Ask an expert. Want to chat? Join a real-time chat. Looking for message boards? You'll find ten different ones, including boards for pets, dogs, cats, fish, birds, and other pets. Registration is required, but it's free. This active online community also includes a large selection of free Pet Vine newspapers—each packed with enlightening articles.

PETSFORUM
http://www.petsforum.com

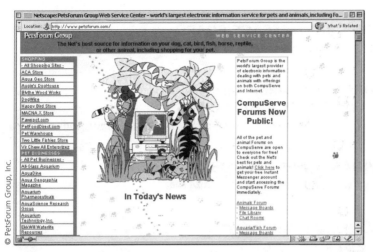

This site offers a free gateway to several live chats and a slew of message boards through Compuserve. Free registration is required.

DOG PRO—ONLINE VET BOARD
http://www.dogpro.com/designs/vetbbs/newvetboard.html

DOG PRO—DOG SHOW AND OBEDIENCE BOARD
http://www.dogpro.com/designs/bbs/wwwboard.html

DOG CHAT MESSAGE FORUM
http://www.dogchat.co.uk

🛒 ACME PET COMMUNITY
FROM PETSMART.COM
http://acmepet.petsmart.com

PETsMART offers live regular chats, vet expert chats, and active message boards.

CAT CHAT MESSAGE BOARD
http://members2.boardhost.com/CatChat

DOG CHAT MESSAGE BOARD
http://members.boardhost.com/dogchat

HORSE WEB DIRECTORY—
NEWSGROUPS AND FORUMS
http://www.horseweb.com/links/Newsgroups_Forums/index.htm

AQUARIA WEB FORUMS
http://www.aquaworldnet.com/awf.htm

E-MAIL LISTS

A **mailing list** is a forum in which participants subscribe to and receive messages by e-mail.

Most e-mail lists are free, and you can subscribe to as many as you please. They come in two main flavors: announcement and discussion. **Announcement lists** (also called newsletters) are one-way and are mainly used to distribute information or news. **Discussion lists** are interactive, allowing the free exchange of messages among list members. These are the lists on which you can ask questions, share stories, and help others with advice.

E-mail discussion groups are moderated, unmoderated, open, or closed. Messages sent to a **moderated list** are first screened before being sent to everyone on the list. This is to keep the messages on topic and prevent "flame wars"—disruptive disagreements between list members. Messages to an **unmoderated list** are not screened. An **open list** welcomes anyone to join. A **closed list** can refer to different things, but it generally means you need approval by the list moderator to join. In most cases, a simple letter stating you want to join generally grants approval.

E-mail lists are capable of producing a lot of e-mail— 30, 40, even 100 or more messages daily. Unless you like that much e-mail, subscribe to a digest version of a list whenever available. A **digest** is a collection of 20 or more messages (depending on the message length) sent to you within a single e-mail.

To subscribe to any e-mail list, you first send a request to a list manager. Some Web sites makes this very easy— you click a button and use an online form to subscribe, unsubscribe, suspend your mail while on vacation, or receive a digest of the list. Other Web sites for popular mail lists instruct you on how to e-mail the list manager. For example, you may send a message to <listmanger@xyz.com> and the body of your letter may say <subscribe digest>. Shortly after you subscribe, you will receive a welcome e-mail from the list manager. Save this important letter as it includes the e-mail address needed to send messages to everyone on the list, the general rules of the list, and instructions on how to unsubscribe from the list. Remember to send your sub-scribe and unsubscribe requests only to the list manager, not the entire group of subscribers.

Keep in mind that you don't have to participate in dis-cussions when you join a list. You can simply read the messages. This is known as **lurking**. Often it's a good idea to lurk to get a sense of the group before posting. You may feel very comfortable with the list and jump into posting. Or, you may find the list isn't what you had in mind, in which case you can unsubscribe.

 *Free*
Mailing Lists

HOFLIN DOG MAILING LISTS
http://www.hoflin.com/Lists/DogLists.html

Select a dog breed, insert your e-mail address, and click a button to subscribe to one of several moderated lists for specific dog breeds.

COMPLETE LIST OF DOG-RELATED MAILING LISTS COMPILED BY CINDY TITTLE MOORE
http://www.k9web.com/dog-faqs/lists/email-list.html

Cindy compiled a vast selection of links and instructions for general, topical, activity-specific, multiple-breed, and specific breed mailing lists.

OFF-LEASH DOG MAILING LIST
http://www.freeplay.org/phplib/fplist.phtml

An informative list for people wanting to share their off-leash dog park efforts and experiences.

CAT FANCIERS MAILING LIST
http://www.fanciers.com/about.html

OTHER CAT-RELATED MAILING LISTS FROM CAT FANCIERS
http://www.fanciers.com/lists.html

Mimy Sluiter last compiled this extensive directory to cat-related mailing lists.

PARROT TALK CONNECTION MAILING LISTS
http://www.parrottalk.com/mlist1.html

PET BIRD MAILING LISTS FROM UP AT SIX AVIARIES
http://www.upatsix.com/lists

CONURES—THE MAILING LIST
http://www.ddc.com/petplace/conurelist

MAILING LISTS FROM THE HAY NET
http://www.haynet.net/Mailing_Lists

An extensive link directory to horse and equestrian-related mailing lists.

AQUATIC ANIMALS MAILING LIST
http://www.actwin.com/fish/lists.html

A collection of mailing lists and subscription information for various aquarium topics.

HORSE WEB—MAILING LISTS
http://www.horseweb.com/links/Listservs

Free Chats

CHAT AT ACME PETS
http://acmepet.petsmart.com/chat

PETCO'S "ASK THE VET" LIVE CHAT
http://www.petco.com/pages/ip_serv_av.html

CYBER PET CHAT
http://www.cyberpetchat.com

BOW WOW YAHOO! CLUBS
http://clubs.yahoo.com/clubs/bowwow

PAT'S PAGE OF DOG CHATS
http://www.doginfomat.com/chats/index.htm

THE HORSE WEB — CHAT ROOMS
http://www.horseweb.com/links/Chat_Rooms

FREE WEBRINGS FOR PET LOVERS

A **WebRing** is a collection of sites linked together by a common theme to form a circle. Traveling a Ring is a great way to discover related sites without having to weed through the quagmire of search engine results. Like jumping from horse to horse on a merry-go-round, you travel a Ring by clicking a navigation link within the Ring's graphic, usually found on the bottom of a member site. Some Rings allow you to view all of the linked sites, others allow you to view five sites at a time, or you can click "next" and travel the Ring until you end up where you started. You don't have to be a member of the ring to travel it, and WebRings are free.

This Adorable Dogs site is owned by Your name.

Want to join the Adorable Dogs webring?

[Skip Prev | Prev | Next]
[Skip Next | Random | Next 5 | List Sites]

ADORABLE DOGS WEB RING
(http://notendur.centrum.is/~sih/adorabledogs.html)

This Happiness is Being Owned by Cats site belongs to **Be-Mi-Kitties**

[Next] [Next5]
[Previous] [Previous 5]
[Random] [List Sites]

[Click here to Join!]

HAPPINESS IS BEING OWNED BY CATS
(http://www.bemikitties.com/webring.htm)

The best way to discover WebRings for pet lovers is to visit **Yahoo! WebRings (http://dir.webring.yahoo.com)**, a master directory of WebRings. My search on *pets* resulted in over 530 Rings; a search on *dogs* over 500 Rings; *cats* over 400; *birds* over 130; *fish* over 300. Of course you can search for any type of Ring you desire. Another popular WebRing for pets is **The Pet Ring (http://www.albritons.com/petring)**.

This Aquaria Web Ring site is owned by Michael Wells

[Previous 5 Sites | Previous | Next | Next 5 Sites | Random Site | List Sites]

Copyright © 2000 by AquaWorld Network

A visit to the **Aquaria Web Ring (http://www.aquaworldnet. com/joinawr.htm)** *will connect you to over 80 other fish-related sites. To travel the Ring, simply click one of the navigation links within the bottom area of the graphic.*

> In order to participate in live chats with other pet lovers, you need to be running an up-to-date browser with Java enabled. In **Netscape**, select **Edit/Preferences** from the menu. A dialog box will appear. Select **Advanced** from the left column. In the main portion of the dialog box, click to place checkmarks next to **Enable Java** and **Enable JavaScript**. Click **OK**. In **Internet Explorer**, select **Edit/Preferences** from the menu. A dialog box will appear. Select **Web Browser** and **Java** from the left column. In the main portion of the dialog box, click to place a checkmark next to **Enable Java**. Click **OK**.

free Veterinary Help, Pet Care, and Nutritional Guidance

Does your puppy need vitamins? How can you stop your hamster's chewing? How should you treat your pet should it ingest antifreeze? What qualifications should you look for in a vet? These questions and many others are answered through the sites in this chapter, which will help you become better informed on caring for your pets and better prepared for any emergency that your pets may face. Remember, "Your veterinarian is the best source of health advice for an individual pet," as Michael Richards, DVM, and Michael Justis of **Vet Info** (**http://www.vetinfo.com**) succinctly state. Visit the Web for general advice and information; visit your vet for specific help.

VETERINARY MEDICINE FROM ABOUT.COM
http://vetmedicine.about.com

Janet Tobiassen Crosby is your host to veterinary medicine on the Web. She shares news, a multitude of links and resources, and feature articles on topics such as pets and fireworks, pool alert, and giving aspirin to pets. Subscribe to the free weekly Veterinary Net News *and join in discussion groups.*

PET HEALTH LIBRARY
FROM OAKS VETERINARY HOSPITALS
http://www.oaksvet.com/pethealthlibrary

A vast collection of articles written by the vets at Oaks Veterinary Hospitals. Categories include health maintenance, older pets, exotics and other pets, parasites and related diseases, miscellaneous problems, and behavior. A new feature, such as arthritis and current treatments, is added monthly.

PET PLACE.COM
http://www.petplace.com

Dr. Jon Rappaport is founder of this exceptional online resource designed to educate pet owners with the latest news and health information. Read top-rated articles in a broad range of topics for dogs, cats, birds, horses, small mammals, reptiles, and fish. Or, use the search engine to sift through more than 700 articles prepared by top veterinarians from places like Angell Memorial Animal Hospital and the Tufts School of Veterinary Medicine to help you locate exactly what you need. If desired, you can complete a short pet-specific profile and receive a personalized Optimal Wellness Program. Find-A-Shelter and Find-A-Hotel databases are included.

BANFIELD, THE PET HOSPITAL
http://www.vetsmart.com

Head over to the FAQ area to read answers to common questions received at Banfield relating to dogs, cats, birds, reptiles, and small and furry pets.

Looking for a vet?
Tap into **Locate a Vet**
(**http://www.locate-a-vet.com**) for a search engine that will assist you in locating a veterinarian anywhere in the United States.

WALTHAM—THE WORLD'S LARGEST AUTHORITY ON PET CARE AND NUTRITION
http://www.waltham.com

For over 65 years Waltham has dedicated itself to improving the health, longevity and happiness of pets. The site is brimming with information and articles on horses, birds, fish, cats, and dogs.

CAT AND DOG CARE FROM THE VETERINARY LIBRARY AT VET NET
http://home.vet.net
http://www.veterinarylibrary.com/main_dogcatcare.htm

This online educational center offers a broad range of topics from internal and external parasites to diseases and dental care. There is also preventive care, nutrition, and health care tips, and related guidance.

AMERICAN ANIMAL HOSPITAL ASSOCIATION— YOUR LINK FOR HEALTHY PETS
http://www.healthypet.com

Is it okay to feed your dog carrots? What is dry eye? Is it okay for your dog to eat grass? Visit Frequently Asked Questions where you'll find answers to these and other questions about behavior, general health, diseases, and miscellaneous pet care. The Pet Care Library includes a wide selection of articles on behavior, common health problems, human/animal bond, nutrition, pet care tips, and preventive care. The Hospital Locator will help you locate an AAHA-accredited veterinary hospital near you or a place you're traveling to.

DR. LARRY PETVET.COM
http://www.drlarrypetvet.com

Submit a question to Dr. Larry or read the question and answer archive. You'll find terrific features on being a good owner, children and pets, and pet health. Other article topics include hip dysplasia, pet insurance, laser surgery, and choosing your pet's veterinarian. Be sure to bookmark Emergency Medical Manual (**http://www.drlarrypetvet.com/health_manual.html**) *for information on chemical burns, choking, fractures, toxins, and other emergencies.*

Did you know that chocolate can be toxic to pets? Or that teflon toxicity occurs most often in pet birds? The **National Animal Poison Control Center** (**http://www.napcc.aspca.org**) recommends that you always be prepared by keeping the number of your veterinarian, a local emergency veterinarian, and the ASPCA National Animal Poison Control Center number (1-888-4 ANI-HELP) in a convenient location. This site includes how you can help prevent indoor, outdoor, and general small animal poisonings and what to do if your pet become poisoned despite of your best efforts to prevent it. Visit **A Pet Owner's Guide to Common Small Animal Poisons** (**http://www.avma.org/pubhlth/poisgde.html**) from The American Veterinary Medical Association to learn about plant, drug, household products, and other items that can be toxic to your pets.

🛒 DOCTORS FOSTER AND SMITH™
PET EDUCATION
http://www.PetEducation.com

Claiming to be the Net's largest and most comprehensive site for pet care, you'll find hundreds of articles on pet health care written by veterinary experts. A pet FAQ, veterinary dictionary, the latest news, free e-mail Dog Care Today or Cat Care Today newsletters, search engine, and other helpful resources are available.

PET CARE FROM THE ASPCA
http://www.aspca.org/learn/petcare.html

The ASPCA provides a variety of resources to help maintain a positive relationship between pet owners and their pets. Get answers to questions about a wide variety of animals and learn how to improve your pet's behavior.

VALUABLE ADVICE FROM SHERLOCK BONES®
http://www.sherlockbones.com/html/advice.html

Learn how to protect your pet from being lost or stolen; helpful hints for finding your lost pet; what to do if you find a wandering pet; and handy information for medical emergencies such as insect bites, heat stroke, burns, seizures, and choking. This information is courtesy of Sherlock Bones®, the tracer of missing pets.

HOMEVET MEDICAL CENTER
http://www.homevet.com

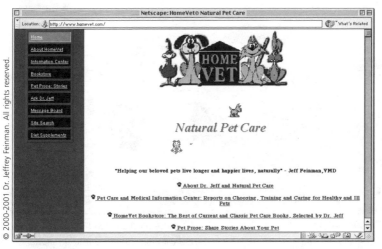

HomeVet is a homeopathic veterinary practice owned and operated by Dr. Jeffrey Feinman of Connecticut. The site's Information Center offers articles on new pets—such as introducing your pet to a new baby, training your pet to tolerate children, and training your child to be pet-wise; sick pets, including cancer links; and natural pet care, including homeopathy, acupuncture, and diet. The site also includes an active message board and pet stories. You can also ask Dr. Jeff a question—for free or a fee.

PET CARE FROM HSUS
http://www.hsus.org/programs/companion/pet_care/pet_care.html

This exceptional collection of feature articles from The Humane Society of the United States includes guidelines for finding a responsible home for a pet; choosing a boarding kennel; choosing a pet sitter; affording veterinary costs; caring for an injured stray; being prepared for disaster, and additional insights.

PROTECT YOUR PET FROM COMMON HOUSEHOLD DANGERS
http://www.hsus.org/programs/companion/pet_care/household_da
ngers.html

VET INFO
http://www.vetinfo.com

Dr. Michael Richards and Michal Justis share numerous dog and cat resources, including canine and feline medical encyclopedias and an alphabetical index of dog and cat healthcare and behavioral information. Learn the qualifications your vet should possess, read tips for choosing a pet, tips from readers, and answers to questions such as, "How do I teach my dog to ride in a car without getting sick?" If you'd like to keep up with the latest in veterinary health care information, a subscription to a monthly newsletter and the ability to ask Dr Mike questions via e-mail is available for a low yearly fee.

PET CARE FROM THE LOST DOGS' HOME ONLINE SHOP
http://www.lostdogshome.org.au

Articles include caring for your dog, cat, puppy, or kitten, as well as responsible pet ownership, and related guidance.

INFORMATION FOR PARENTS ABOUT CHILD-PET INTERACTIONS
http://views.vcu.edu/paws/info.htm

FEMA—ANIMALS AND ANIMAL EMERGENCIES
http://www.fema.gov/fema/anemer.htm

CARE FOR PETS
http://www.avma.org/care4pets

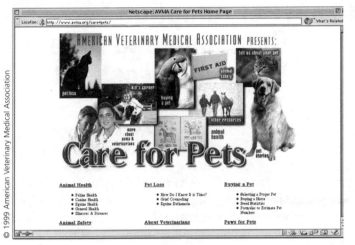

American Veterinary Medical Association offers articles on pet loss—including grief counseling, buying a pet, animal safety, animal health information, pet stories, pet health in the news, and other resources, such as how to select a veterinarian.

PET BEHAVIOR CLINIC
http://www.pethelp.net

Learn how to reduce and eliminate problem pet behavior through interpretation and behavior modification. There are plenty of techniques for dogs, cats, and other pets. Also included is information on wild life, pet adoption, losing a pet, ethics, and animal training.

free Pet Adoption Guidance and Help Locating a Lost Pet

The sight of a homeless domestic animal is heartbreaking. Contrary to popular belief, domestic animals cannot fend for themselves. If left to do so, they will either meet a violent death, a slow, painful death, or will enter a shelter. **The American Society for the Prevention of Cruelty to Animals** (**http://www.aspca.org/adopt**) states that "each year up to 60% of dogs and up to 70% of cats that enter shelters will end up dying because there is no one to adopt them." That translates to millions of dogs and cats per year. If you are ready to enhance your life with a pet, please visit the sites in this chapter to learn how you can adopt one from a rescue group or shelter. These animals want to be loved, and they will love in return. If you are looking for a specific breed, you'll find many breed rescue groups that will be more than happy to accommodate you. If your lifestyle is active and you don't have the time to train a puppy or kitten, consider adopting an older pet—generally housetraining and teething stages are over, they are more settled, and dogs are used to being walked with a leash. If you lost or found an animal, or can no longer keep your pet for whatever reason, there are several sites that can quickly connect you to resources for help.

There are many exceptional organizations that work very hard at placing animals in loving homes. Several sites in this chapter will point you toward specific ones. For more Web resources, see **Animal Organizations and Causes** (**http://www.animalden.net/animalorg.htm**) from Animal Den® and **Net Vet Animal Welfare/Rights/Humane/Rescue Organizations** (**http://netvet.wustl.edu/welfare.htm**).

PET FINDER
http://www.petfinder.org

Thousands of adoptable pets from a staggering number of shelters are featured at this astounding site. Post a free ad for a lost, found, or wanted pet. Visit the Library for articles on adoption, animal care, awareness, behavior, disaster planning, feral cats, travel, and more. Use the Nearby Shelters searchable database to locate animal welfare organizations near you; the Pet Search Plus engine to help you locate the pet you'd like to adopt; or the Breed Index to view thousands of birds, cats, dogs, horses, pigs, rabbits, reptiles, and small and furry creatures available for adoption. There are also several discussion boards where you can learn from an expert or share your experience.

HOW TO FIND A LOST DOG OR CAT
http://www.petrescue.com/library/find-pet.htm

This valuable article from **The Pet Action League** (**http://www.petrescue.com**) details ways to help find your lost dog or cat, including words of caution such as: never respond to a "found" pet contact alone. The article also includes information on protecting your pet now to help ensure that you can be located if your pet is later lost.

MISSING PET NETWORK
http://www.missingpet.net

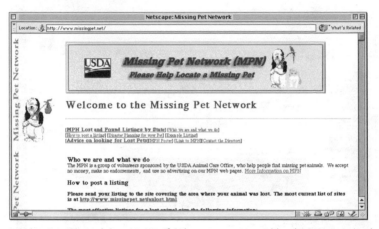

Missing Pet Network is a group of volunteers sponsored by the USDA Animal Care Office who help people find missing pets. Visit this site to post a free listing for any missing pet—not just dogs and cats—to the MPN volunteer listed for your state (Canadian and the Netherlands postings are also accepted). There's a special page for horses, too. Or view the lost and found listings. Be sure to read *Finding a Lost Pet—Where to Start* (**http://www.missing pet.net/advice/index.html**) for excellent guidance. A free poster is available to help spread the word about the Missing Pet Network.

PET SHELTER NETWORK
http://www.petshelter.org

The Pet Shelter Network is an on-line network of nationwide animal shelters and rescue organizations whose primary goal is in helping to place homeless dogs and cats. Complete a pet profile at the Adoption Center, click a button, and you are provided with a listing of available matches with descriptions and shelter info. The Be Smart section includes articles on what you need to know about adopting a pet, including the adoption process. If you need to find a new home for your pet, the HomeFinder section can help. If you lost or found a pet, let the world know by posting a free message.

HUGS FOR HOMELESS ANIMALS
http://www.h4ha.org

Hugs for Homeless Animals is dedicated to providing comfort to homeless and displaced animals awaiting placement in good homes. The site includes a vast worldwide shelter directory and a free worldwide lost and found pets section. Visit the Hugs Road- house to participate in message boards, real-time chat, read poems and stories, or listen to music. Related resources are included.

FIDONYC
http://fidonyc.org

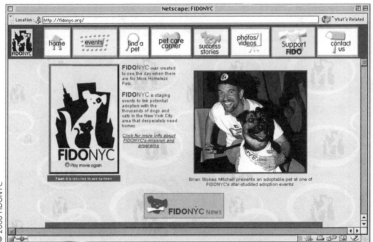

Bernadette Peters and Mary Tyler Moore created FIDONYC with director Stacey Shub. Tap into this site to learn about the thousands of dogs and cats in the New York City area that desperately need homes.

KITTY VILLAGE
http://www.kittyvillage.org

The primary purpose of Kitty Village is to match people who want to adopt a cat with cat rescuers, humane societies, and owners—but not breeders. The site also includes links to feline- related articles from leading U.S. newspapers and additional links to stories from around the Net.

PET PROMISE
http://www.petpromise.org

*This organization located in Columbus, OH is dedicated to the res-
cue and placement of homeless cats, dogs, kittens, and puppies in
Ohio, Indiana, and surrounding states. "Can We Help You Keep
Your Pet?"* (**http://www.petpromise.org/surrenderhelp.html**) *
includes articles such as Introducing a New Baby to your Dog/Cat;
Taking Control of Allergies; and Responsible Guidelines to Placing
Your Pet. You'll find plenty of dog and cat guidance information
and many resources, too.*

**Wondering how you can help pet shelters in
your neighborhood?** One way to find out is to call
and ask. Another is to visit the **Pet Food Bank.org**
(**http://www.petfoodbank.org**). Click on the "How can I
help?" button, select a location you'd most like to help,
then learn about shelters that need your assistance. In
addition to monetary donations, shelters often need
things like paper towels, pet food, blankets, sheets, and
bath towels.

HEARTS UNITED FOR ANIMALS—AUBURN, NE
http://www.hua.org

Hearts United for Animals is a national shelter, sanctuary, and animal welfare organization where there are no cages, but rather large fenced fields where the pets can play. Dogs and cats that cannot be adopted stay as "Sanctuary Sweethearts" for their remaining lives. Visit this site to learn about the organization and how you can help support it.

RESCUERS.ORG
http://www.rescuers.org

*Whether you are looking to adopt a new pet, need to find a home for a pet, or have a concern about animal welfare, tap into this site for a extensive listing of Rescues and Shelters By State (**http://www.rescuers.org/links1.htm***) and Breed Specific Rescues (**http://www.rescuers.org/links2.htm***).*

WWW SHELTERS ONLINE
http://www.nhspca.org/online.html

An alphabetized listing of shelters, organized by state and with links to their Web site, courtesy of the New Hampshire SPCA.

BREED RESCUE ORGANIZATIONS, PART 1–PART 4, FROM REC.PETS.DOG

http://faqs.jmas.co.jp/FAQs/dogs-faq/rescue/part1
http://faqs.jmas.co.jp/FAQs/dogs-faq/rescue/part2
http://faqs.jmas.co.jp/FAQs/dogs-faq/rescue/part3
http://faqs.jmas.co.jp/FAQs/dogs-faq/rescue/part4

This extensive canine rescue organizations list was compiled from the rec.pets.dogs Usenet group by Janice Ritter. Breed-specific organizations are listed first, followed by all-breed and specialty organizations.

PET FRIENDS ANIMAL SANCTUARY—KANAB, UT
http://www.bestfriends.org

Take a video or photo tour of the nation's largest sanctuary for abused and abandoned dogs, cats, and other animals. The site includes much for all pet lovers to read and explore, including a weekly newsletter, feature articles, Best Friends Magazine (free past issues available), a pets forum, and related information.

If you find an injured animal, do you know what to do? Visit The Wildlife Rehabilitation Information Directory (**http://www.tc.umn.edu/~devo0028**) from Ronda DeVold. Her site is a resource on what to do and who to contact. Be sure to read "Wild Animals As Pets? Why the Answer is Always No."

---

free Help for Dog Lovers

I confess: I am a doe-eyed-with-admiration, dog-loving, dog person. Blame it on Mustang, my beloved pooch who is mainly Labrador with a pinch of German Shepherd—a 50+ pound black bundle of canine perfection with a large white dignified spot on his chest—who came into my life almost 13 years ago. Blame it on his perfect little face and whimsical expressions, his staunch loyalty, and the way he treats me like I am the most important person in the world. His daily dose of unconditional love consistently warms my soul while melting away life's little irritations. Without saying a word, Mustang continually teaches me how extraordinary dogs are. And if the number of dog-related Web sites is any indication, there are zillions of other dog lovers out there. This chapter contains a mere sampling of the larger, dog-related sites on the Web that will amuse, delight, and answer your general questions.

To locate additional dog-related Web sites, visit the **rec. pets.dogs FAQ Homepage (http://www.k9web.com/dog-faqs)**, which includes a massive list of links and answers to your dog-related questions compiled by Cindy Tittle Moore from the rec.pets.dogs Usenet group. Other large directories of dog-related sites include: **The Dog Infomat (http://www.doginfo mat.com)**; All About Dogs **(http://allaboutdogs.com)**; Dog Seek **(http://www.dogseek.com)**; Professor Hunt's Dog Page **(http://www.cofc.edu/~huntc/dogpage.html)** and Dogmark— Cool Dog Site of the Day **(http://www.dogmark.net)**.

DOGS AT ABOUT.COM
http://dogs.about.com

Thinking of buying your youngster a spotted puppy? First read "What's wrong with 102 Dalmations," one of several features by T.E. Ellis, your About.com guide to dogs. Ellis also shares dog essentials—such as breed profiles, dog basics, housetraining your dog, and preventing dog bites—a multitude of resources, and a free newsletter.

DOG.COM
http://www.dog.com

You'll find top dog-related news headlines, articles, a free downloadable doggie screensaver, and a searchable database to over 12,400 dog-related Web sites.

THE DOG PATCH
http://www.dogpatch.org/dogs

Bursting with a wealth of resources, this is one of the largest canine sites on the Web. Visit Dogpatch Articles to read about canine CPR, poisonous plants, hints on photographing your dog, and other topics.

DOG INFO MAT
http://www.doginfomat.com

Extensive dog-related articles, features, photos, and a categorized collection of resources.

CYBER-DOG
http://www.cyberpet.com/cyberdog

Cyber-Dog's mission is to provide you with umpteen informative articles in topics such as finding a pet, health and nutrition, behavior, rescue, dog showing, and general advice. Also available are resources to dog breeds, breeders, rescue organizations, and a breed information database.

SAM AND ME.COM
http://www.samandme.com

This Web community invites you to create a free Web page of your pooch, share your dog story, and send a free doggie e-card to others.

NEW PET HOME PAGE
http://www.newpet.com/main/index.htm

Wondering how much it really costs to own and care for a dog? Tap into vast resources for new or soon-to-be dog owners to find the answer to this and other questions.

PURINA® PUPPY CHOW—COMPLETE PUPPY NUTRITION AND CARE INFORMATION
http://www.puppychow.com

Purina® offers valuable information on feeding, health, training, behavior, and nutrition. Sign up for a free puppy care kit that includes a video and puppy care booklet. You can also sign up for a free e-mail newsletter, download free puppy wallpaper for your computer desktop, or send your friends a free puppy postcard.

DOGSITES—FOR ALL THINGS CANINE
http://www.dogsites.com.au

Tips on training, information on responsible dog ownership, health issues, breed profiles, and more from this Australian site.

Dogs and Children

HOW TO LOVE YOUR DOG— A KID'S GUIDE TO DOG CARE
http://www.howtoloveyourdog.com

Janet Wall shares over 80 topics and 200 pages of information focusing on kindness, commitment, and teaching responsible dog care to children around the world. Kids can also submit their own stories for online publication.

DOG PERFECT
http://www.dogperfect.com

Sarah Hodgon offers guidance on choosing a dog, quarterly tips on caring and training your dog, and an active message board.

DOGGIE FUN
http://www.doggiefun.com

*Read articles, sign up for a free newsletter, submit your dog photos to The Dog Park, and visit **DoggieTalk** (**http://www.doggiefun .com/discus**)—where you'll find an assortment of forums to discuss your doggie's needs. Plenty of related resources are included.*

KIDS AND DOGS SAFETY TIP SHEET BY SHEILA BLYTHE-SAUCIER
http://petwalk.com/articles/kids_safety.htm

Sheila offers 15 safety guidelines to teach children, such as never run up to a dog.

KIDS AND DOGS—A COMMON SENSE APPROACH FROM DOG OWNER'S GUIDE
http://www.canismajor.com/dog/kidsdog2.html

Read this award-winning comprehensive article by Vicki DeGruy that includes extensive links and resources.

KIDS AND DOGS FROM CHESAPEAKE BAY RETRIEVER RELIEF & RESCUE
http://www.cbrrescue.org/kids_and_dogs.htm

Wally Clay explains from a personal perspective how to integrate a new dog into the home.

ADDING A NEW BABY TO THE PET HOUSEHOLD BY DIANA GUERRERO
http://www.cyberpet.com/cyberdog/articles/behavior/ addbaby.htm

PURINA® DOG CHOW—
YOUR GUIDE TO INCREDIBLE DOGS
http://www.dogchow.com

Learn everything from preparing your home and setting a routine to caring for your older, pregnant, or hardworking dogs. Free postcards, wallpaper for your computer desktop, and other valuable info are available at this site from Purina®.

THE DOG AGILITY PAGE
http://www.dogpatch.org/agility

Dog agility is a non-regimented sport in which a handler is given a certain amount of time to direct a dog without a leash through an obstacle course of jumps, tunnels, weave poles, etc. This site offers a large selection of articles, forums, clubs, links, events and more—all related to dog agility.

DOGS IN THE ARTS
http://www.uncc.edu/jvanoate/k9/artdogs.htm

Judith Van Noate designed and maintains this large collection of resources that celebrates the image of dogs in art, literature, theater, television, and the Web.

> Send the favorite people in your life a doggie e-card. Visit these sites:
>
> Dog-o-Grams (**http://woofmail.com**),
> Funny Post Cards Featuring Dog Pictures
> (**http://www.funnypostcard.com**),
> and Barking Buddy Postcards
> (**http://www.barkingbuddies.com/postcard2.html**)

🛒 PAWGEAR.COM
http://www.pawgear.com

*You'll find plenty of canine information here, including articles and dog-related news, the K-9 Chat Café, and PawGear—a discussion board. Want a dog screensaver? You'll find some here to download. Be sure to visit the Dog Ownership Guide (**http://www.pawgear.com/information/dogownership/ index.html**) which covers topics such as yard safety, making a first aid bag, and caring for senior dogs.*

DOG O MANIA
http://www.dogomania.com

Mega dog-related links, resources, and articles.

THE SENIOR DOGS PROJECTS
http://www.srdogs.com

Dedicated to the senior dog, be sure to visit the How to Care for an Older Dog page for exceptional guidance on everything from aging signs and alternative medicine to stroke and vestibular disease.

DOG HOBBYIST
http://www.doghobbyist.com

This information portal for the canine enthusiast offers weekly news, chats, and plenty of forums.

DOG-PLAY—HAVING FUN WITH YOUR DOG
http://www.dog-play.com

Diane Blackman hosts this exceptional site featuring many fun activities that people can do with their dogs.

MIGHTY DOG—YOUR SMALL DOG RESOURCE
http://www.mightydog.com/home.asp

Did you know that small dogs use twice the energy as large dogs do? Read this article from Friskies®, makers of Mighty Dog.

PEPPY POOCH
http://www.peppypooch.com

Peppy Pooch offers quality information on holistic dog health care, entertaining stories, resources, and related info.

CHAPTER 7

Dog Behavior and Training Advice

Tired of dispensing commands that your pooch pays no heed to? Wondering how to teach your cantankerous canine that you are the alpha male? If you don't have the time or budget to enroll in dog training classes, tap into the Web. It is replete with sites offering guidance on how you can help your dog overcome common behavior problems, and many sites are particularly helpful to new puppy owners. Remember when training your dog, avoid aggression; it begets aggression. Instead, treat your dog gently and humanely and use consistent and positive reinforcement. With time and patience, disagreeable canine behavior can be corrected. Your dog will become a more pleasant companion, and you can take pride in being a responsible and loving owner. The sites in this chapter will help you learn how.

DR. P'S DOG TRAINING
http://www.uwsp.edu/psych/dog/dog.htm

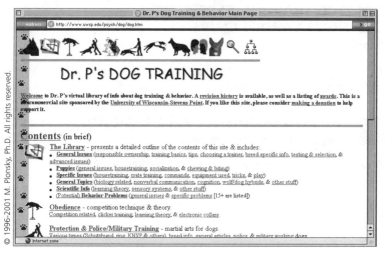

An abundant selection of articles and resources from Dr. Plonsky, a psychology professor with a passionate interest in dog training.

TRAINING YOUR DOG
http://www.learnfree.com/dog/default.htm

Free online videos that teach basic dog obedience exercises, such as sit, stay, come, heel, leash training, crate training, and other exercises—from Learnfree.com.

DOGGIE LOGIC OBEDIENCE PAGE
http://www.doglogic.com/obedmain.htm

This library of articles includes crate, leash, attention, and other training and obedience techniques.

 ## DOG PROBLEMS.COM
http://www.dogproblems.com

Adam Katz offers articles, product information, a free weekly dog training tips e-zine, and more—all designed to help you fix your dog training problems.

 ## DOG TRAINING FORUM
http://www.dogforum.com

Tap into this site to discuss dog training techniques, find training resources, or just chat.

DOG TRAINING EXPERIENCES FROM YAHOO! CLUBS
http://clubs.yahoo.com/clubs/dogtrainingexperiences

This active club includes a chat room and message boards for anyone wanting to share their experiences related to dog training.

THE DOG OBEDIENCE AND TRAINING PAGE
http://www.dogpatch.org/obed

A portal to basic training, competitive obedience, clubs and schools, clicker training, and other resources and links.

"CANINE TO FIVE"
DOGGY DAYCARE AND TRAINING FACILITY
http://www.canine2five.com

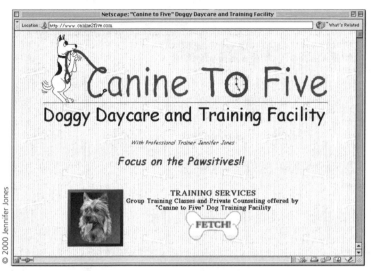

Jennifer Jones specializes in terrior behavior and training, and she offers excellent information for all dog owners. Topics include methods of learning, common behavior problems and solutions, general advice for puppies, training equipment, and more.

CANINES.COM—
WORLD OF DOGS AND TRAINING
http://www.canines.com

This site is loaded with many articles, resources, and information for dealing with specific troublesome behaviors, such as excessive barking, territorial aggression, chewing, and digging. I found the article, "When Spot is Hot, Pets in Parked Cards Can Be a Deadly Mistake" particularly provoking.

DOG BITE PREVENTION
http://www.avma.org/press/dogbite/dogbitebroc.asp

The American Veterinary Medical Association explains that even the cuddliest, fuzziest, sweetest pup can bite if provoked. Learn how to avoid being bitten and what to do if your dog bites someone.

🛒 PERFECT PAWS—
DOG AND CAT TRAINING AND BEHAVIOR CENTER
http://www.perfectpaws.com

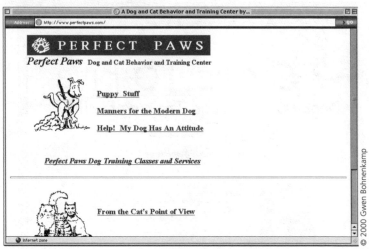

This site features extensive information from Gwen Bohnenkamp's two books: Manners for the Modern Dog, which includes down-to-earth advice on housetraining, barking, chewing, digging, separation anxiety, and much more and Help! My Dog Has An Attitude, which covers the causes, cures and prevention of attitude problems in pet dogs. If you like the information, order the books. Additional guidance on training your puppy is included.

DOG GROOMING FROM SUITE 101
http://www.suite101.com/welcome.cfm/dog_grooming

Chris Chamberlin explains how grooming is essential for maintaining your dog's health and happiness.

DOG TRAINING BASICS
http://www.ddc.com/petplace/dogtraining

Professional dog trainer, Pam Young, shares her training secrets in a series of articles designed to help you keep the upperhand with your canine companion. Articles include why won't my dog listen to me, the proper way to use commands, and taking control of the food bowl.

🛒 DOG LOGIC
http://www.doglogic.com

While geared primarily to Great Danes, its extensive training and health information, including emergency first aid tips, apply to all dogs.

AMERICAN DOG TRAINERS NETWORK
http://www.canine.org

Robin Kovar shares resources and articles, including how to choose a dog trainer, how we cause our dogs to misbehave, cold and hot weather safety tips, canines in the car, twelve tips for a well-behaved dog.

DOGGIE DOOR—THE INTERNET'S "DOGGIE DOOR TO CANINE BEHAVIOR"
http://www.doggiedoor.com

This site features twelve main topics, including separation anxiety, house training, and aggression. Each is organized with a list of questions to help you find to answers to your pet's behavior problems. Visit **The Puppy Place** (**http://www.doggiedoor.com/puppy**) *for puppy-related articles.*

DOG TRAINING, DOG PROBLEMS, DOG OBEDIENCE, AND DOG BEHAVIOR
http://www.dogproblems.com

Adam Katz designed his site to help you fix any of the dog training problems you might be experiencing with your dog.

STAY BITE FREE
http://www.nodogbites.org

Humane Society of the U.S. details how proper socialization, supervision, humane training, sterilization, and safe confinement are necessary to prevent dogs from biting. You'll find quick tips, how to bite-proof your dog and yourself, kids' safety tips, and more. Other helpful sites from The Humane Society of the United States include **Dog Care** (**http://www.hsus.org/programs/companion/pet_care/dog_care.html**) *and* Dog Behavior (**http://www.hsus.org/ programs/companion/pet_behavior/ dog_behavior.html**).

free Info on Dog Breeds, Organizations, and Clubs

The Rottweiler is an excellent guard dog. The Siberian Husky, the Rottweiler's antithesis, does not like to bark or guard but is known for its occasional howl and will run and run, if given the chance. The Golden Retriever and Labrador Retriever are quintessential family dogs. The American Hairless Terrier, Poodle, or Bichon, could be ideal for an allergy sufferer. No matter what your lifestyle, there is a dog existing in the world that can be your perfect companion. The sites in this chapter celebrate different dog breeds, including mixed-breeds, and their varying personalities and needs.

Free General Dog Breed Information Sites

YOUR MIXED BREED DOG
http://www.dog-play.com/mixed.html

Diane Blackman offers info and resources on the mixed breed dog, also called a mutt, mixie, or an All American.

THE MIXED BREED DOG
FROM THE DOG OWNER'S GUIDE
http://www.canismajor.com/dog/mixed.html

This thorough article with resources describes the advantages, drawbacks, and temperaments of the mixed-breed dog.

THE DOG BREED ALPHABET
http://www.hos.honden.nl/hondenrassen/dogbreeds.html

HOS (a dog training and behavior modification center in the Netherlands) offers an all-breeds encyclopedia, resources, breed profiles, clubs, photos, and lots more.

DOG BREED INFORMATION CENTER
http://www.dogbreedinfo.com

Search through an A-to-Z listing of dog breeds or by category such as lap dog, reliability with children, reliability with strangers, breeds good for apartment life, or excellent jogging buddies. A fantastic selection of articles on caring for your dog are included.

SPECIFIC BREEDS
http://www.specificbreeds.com

This compendium of dog information includes invaluable guidance on buying a puppy, preparing your home for a new dog, keeping your dog healthy, and info on a canine's tracking ability and its anatomy.

GROUPS AND BREEDS FROM DOG INFOMAT
http://www.doginfomat.com/dog02.htm

*A portal to a categorized collection of dog breed sites, forums, and resources. Be sure to visit **An Introduction to Researching Different Types of Dogs & Finding the Right Source** (**http://www.doginfomat.com/breedsintro.htm**) and **Before You Get A Dog** (**http://www.doginfomat.com/b4ugetadog.htm**), by Sandi Dremel—two excellent sites bursting with valuable information.*

DOG BREEDS FROM PETNET.COM.AU
http://www.petnet.com.au/dogs/dogbreedindex.html

From the Afghan Hound to the Yorkshire Terrier, you'll find information on over 100 dog breeds from this Australian site.

WALTERS & SHACKLES GUIDE TO DOG BREEDS
http://www.gardening-uk.com/dogs/breeds/breed_guide.html

Although designed as a resource for British dog owners, anyone looking for information on dog breeds will appreciate the alphabetized general indexes, including a thorough description and history of each breed. Additional resources are included.

PUPPYFINDER
http://www.puppyfinder.com

Puppyfinder can assist individuals and families in discovering the best breed of dog for their lifestyle. It provides potential sources for their chosen breed, and answers questions online to guide owners through all stages of the dog's life. Also featured are articles in a wide variety of care topics.

BREED FAQ HOMEPAGE
http://www.k9web.com/dog-faqs/breeds

Cindy Tittle Moore presents extensive information, divided by breed, compiled from the rec.pets.dogs Usenet group. Within each breed section you'll find a history, characteristics and temperament, frequently asked questions, and resources.

Free Guidance for Specific Breeds of Dogs

ALASKAN MALAMUTE
http://www.malamute.org

BEAGLES-ON-THE-WEB
http://www.beagles-on-the-web.com

BULLDOG.ORG
http://www.bulldog.org

BULL AND TERRIER
http://www.bullandterrier.com

Heather Steward's site is dedicated to protecting and defending the American Pit Bull Terrier, American Staffordshire Terrier, Staffordshire Bull Terrier, and all other Pit Bull type dogs.

THE COCKER SPANIEL INFORMATION PAGES
http://www.cockerspanielinformation.com

GREAT DANE WELFARE ISSUES
http://www.ginnie.com/welfare.htm

HAPPY HUSKIES
http://www.angelfire.com/on3/happyhuskies/main.html

 ## MALTESE ONLY
http://malteseonly.com

THE POMERANIAN
http://www.geocities.com/~pomerama

PUGS
http://www.pugs.com

SIBERIAN HUSKIES
www.husky-petlove.com/mushing.html

SNOWBEAR GREAT PYRENEES
http://www.snowbear-greatpyrenees.com

SIBERIAN HUSKY CLUB OF AMERICA
http://www.shca.org/shcahp2b.htm

THE DOBERMAN PINSCHER CLUB OF AMERICA
http://www.dpca.org

Free Web Sites of Dog Clubs and Associations

AMERICAN DOG OWNERS ASSOCIATION
http://www.adoa.org

🛒 AMERICAN KENNEL CLUB
http://www.akc.org/index.html

© 2000 The American Kennel Club

This non-profit organization established in 1884 maintains a purebred dog registry, sanctions dog events, and promotes responsible dog ownership. This site features a compendium of resources, including articles, news, and extensive information on dog breeds.

THE KENNEL CLUB
http://www.the-kennel-club.org.uk

WILD DOG FOUNDATION
http://www.wilddog.org

WORLD KENNEL CLUB
http://www.worldkennelclub.com

AMERICAN MIXED BREEDS OBEDIENCE REGISTRATION
http://www.amborusa.org

AMBOR was established in 1983 to acknowledge the efforts and achievements of mixed breed dogs and their handlers in obedience competition, to provide encouragement and support to those handlers, and to affirm the accomplishments of mixed breeds.

THE AMERICAN HAIRLESS TERRIER
http://members.aol.com/AHTerrier/home.html

BEARDED COLLIE CLUB OF AMERICA
http://beardie.net/bcca

BORDER COLLIER SOCIETY OF AMERICA
http://www.BorderCollieSociety.com

BULL TERRIER CLUB OF AMERICA
http://www.btca.com

THE ENGLISH COCKER SPANIEL CLUB OF AMERICA, INC.
http://www.ecsca.org

THE AMERICAN BOXER CLUB
http://clubs.akc.org/abc/abc-home.htm

This official site of the American Boxer Club, maintained by Dr. Calvin D. Gruver and Judy Voran features articles, news, Boxer history, health, and resources.

If you're looking for more guidance in selecting the right dog for your lifestyle, here are more Web sites to peruse:

• Choosing the Perfect Dog
http://www.choosingtheperfectdog.net

• Everything you Wanted to Know About Puppies But Just Forgot to Ask
http://workingdogs.com/30puptipsg.htm

• The Breed Selector from Purina® Dog Chow
http://www.dogchow.com

• Buying A Puppy from the American Kennel Club
http://www.akc.org/love/dah/buyapup.cfm

• Choosing the Right Dog
http://www.dogpark.com/dright.html

• The Dog Breed Selector
http://www.selectsmart.com/DOG

GREYHOUNDS UNLIMITED
http://www.greyhoundsunlimited.org

THE JACK RUSSELL TERRIER CLUB OF AMERICA
http://www.terrier.com

This is the official site for the largest Jack Russell Terrier club and registry in the world. You'll find more than 500 pictures, extensive advice, "Jack Talk," a question and answer forum, and other related information.

THE LABRADOR RETRIEVER CLUB OF AMERICA
http://thelabradorclub.com

GERMAN SHEPHERD DOG CLUB OF AMERICA
http://www.gsdca.org

GOLDEN RETRIEVER CLUB OF AMERICA
http://www.grca.org

THE POODLE CLUB OF AMERICA
http://www.swdg.com/pca

YORKSHIRE TERRIER CLUB OF AMERICA
http://www.ytca.org

Dog Allergies? If you want a dog but are allergic to them, be sure to visit **Allergic to Dogs?** (**http://members.aol.com/AHTerrier/allergies.html**). While no dog is truly non-allergenic, some breeds produce less dander than others. The site features a list of the breeds that allergy sufferers may be able to tolerate, helpful environmental controls such as having floors rather than wall-to-wall carpeting, an interactive discussion board, and helpful resources and links for pet allergy sufferers.

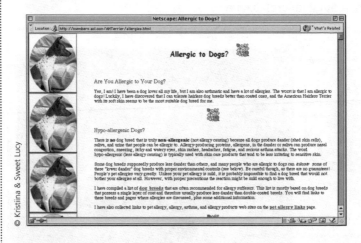

© Kristiina & Sweet Lucy

free Web Sites of Dog Magazines

Many canine magazines host Web sites that include feature articles from the print version of their publication. Some include searchable archives of past articles, message boards, and other forums. There are also "e-zines"—electronic magazines or newsletters—for dog lovers that you can read by visiting the Web site each month or by subscribing to an e-mail list. One of the most impressive e-zines is the *Dog Owners Guide Online Magazine* (**http://www.canismajor.com/dog**). It includes "more than 300 pages of features, breed profiles, training tips, health information, and articles about shelters, rescue, dogs and the law, and just about everything else you need to know about living with your dog."

© 2000 Canis Major Publications

🛒 *Tap into the* Dog Owners Guide Online Magazine (**http://www.canismajor.com/dog**) *for a plethora of dog-related articles and advice.*

Free Web Sites of Dog Magazines

THE GREAT DANE REPORTER
http://www.gdr.com

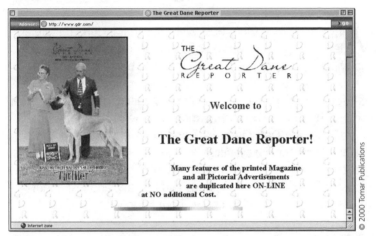

Many articles and some of the most requested reprints from this premiere publication for Great Dane enthusiasts are available at this site.

THE BARK
http://www.thebark.com

DOGS IN REVIEW
http://www.dogsinreview.com

DOG FANCY
http://www.animalnetwork.com/dogs

GOOD DOG MAGAZINE
http://www.gooddogmagazine.com

DOGS IN CANADA
http://www.dogs-in-canada.com

SHELTIE INTERNATIONAL
http://www.sheltieinternational.com

DOG WORLD MAGAZINE
http://www.dogworldmag.com

Dog World Magazine *brings you Dog World Online, the dog lover's Internet source for breeds, training, nutrition, behavior and show information about man's best friend.*

DOG & KENNEL
http://www.dogandkennel.com

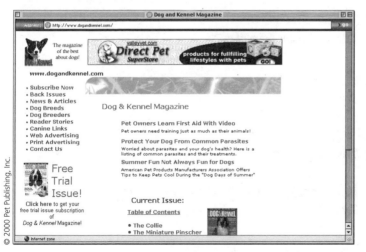

Read news and articles, reader's stories, and sign up for a free trial issue. The site also features dog breed profiles, breeders, and related resources.

Free Web Sites of Dog E-Zines and Newsletters

WORKING DOGS CYBERZINE
http://workingdogs.com

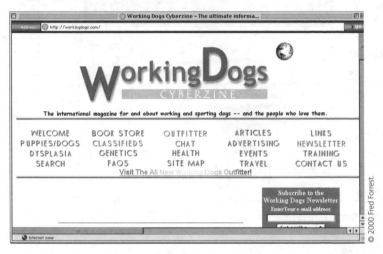

This Cyberzine provides continuously updated info and articles about working and sporting dogs and the people who work, train, breed, and love them.

THE STRAIGHT POOP
http://www.straight-poop.com

DOGDAZE E-ZINE
http://www.dogdaze.com

THE CANINE TIMES
http://www.caninetimes.com

WORLD CLASS DOG MAGAZINE
http://www.worldclassdogs.com/Magazine.asp

SHOW DOG SUPERSITE
http://www.showdogsupersite.com

 🛒 **THE POOP**

http://www.thepoop.com

This mega-friendly impressive site includes The PoopPourri, featuring articles and resources; the Expert Den, where a vet answers questions; the Poop Pantry with recipes your dog will drool over, such as chow-chow chicken, doggy dip, and pooch peanut-butter swirls—and more.

 THE DAILY DOG
http://www.dailydog.com

WDW NEWS
http://www.workingdogweb.com/wdwnews.htm

DOGZONE
http://www.dogzone.com

BARK BYTES—CANINE MAGAZINE
http://www.barkbytes.com

WOOFS
http://www.woofs.org

CANINE TIMES
http://www.cfnaonline.com/caninetimes

Canine Times is a free e-zine you can subscribe to featuring interesting, sometimes funny, sometimes poignant, dog news. Archives are available, or use the search engine to locate articles from past issues.

 DOGS WORLDWIDE
http://www.dogsworldwide.com

 DOG FANCY
http://www.animalnetwork.com/dogs

NYC DOG LIFE
http://www.nycdoglife.com

 A BREED APART—THE FIRST GREYHOUND E-ZINE
http://www.abap.org/framestart.htm

free Info on Dogs that Help Those in Need

After the First World War thousands of guide dogs were trained in Germany to help the war-blinded. Today service dogs can do tasks such as pull a wheelchair, open doors, and turn light switches off and on. Dogs can be trained to help visually impaired, hearing impaired, and other persons with limitations and provide them with dignity, mobility, and greater independence. Dogs can also be trained to help save human life in a disaster. Visit these sites for more information and to help support the various organizations and their efforts.

GUIDE DOGS FOR THE BLIND, INC.
http://www.guidedogs.com

© 1997 Guide Dogs for the Blind, Inc

Established in 1942, Guide Dogs for the Blind provides enhanced mobility to qualified individuals through partnership with dogs whose unique skills are developed and nurtured by dedicated volunteers and a professional staff.

LIVE, LOVE AND LAUGH WITH GOLDEN RETRIEVERS AT THE LAND OF PUREGOLD
http://landofpuregold.com

Rochelle Lesser is a school psychologist actively involved in training Golden Retrievers to be therapy, classroom demonstration, and agility dogs. Her inspiring site celebrates the human-canine bond, supports the belief that "dogs aren't a child's whole life, but that they can make their lives whole," and explores every service field and humanitarian effort that Golden Retrievers are responsible for. Be sure to visit **Golden Opportunities** (**http://landofpuregold. com/wow.htm**) where you can sign up for the Land of PureGold Mailing List, read and share your Golden stories, and participate in other activities.

SERVICE DOGS FROM SUITE 101
http://www.suite101.com/welcome.cfm/service_dogs

Jean Ann Wall offers articles and resources on seizure-alert dogs.

CANINE COMPANIONS FOR INDEPENDENCE
http://www.caninecompanions.org

PAWS WITH A CAUSE
http://www.pawswithacause.org

THERAPY DOG INTERNATIONAL
http://www.tdi-dog.org

DOGS FOR THE DEAF, INC.
http://www.dogsforthedeaf.org

THE GUIDE DOGS FOR THE BLIND ASSOCIATION
http://graphics.gdba.org.uk

GUIDING EYES FOR THE BLIND, INC.
http://www.guiding-eyes.org

GUIDE DOGS OF NEW SOUTH WALES
http://www.guidedogs.com.au

In addition to information about Guide Dogs and the services this organization provides, the site includes online resources for the public such as how to behave towards a guide dog, how to guide a person with a visual impairment, and what to do (and not do) when you meet a blind person.

THE SEEING EYE, INC.
http://www.seeingeye.org

NATIONAL DISASTER SEARCH DOG FOUNDATION
http://www.ndsdf.org

free Help for
Cat Lovers

Affectionate yet obstinate, playful yet dignified, the ever-frisky feline has fascinated humans since ancient times. Whether you color yourself an ailurophile or are pondering the addition of a cat to your home, tapping into the Web can help you better understand and care for your glorious and graceful creature. The sites in this chapter are large and will keep you well-informed and entertained. For more cat-related help and advice, see Chapter 12.

If you have a particular cat question, visit the **rec.pets.cats FAQs Homepage** (**http://www.fanciers.com/cat-faqs/index.html**) maintained by Cindy Tittle Moore. It's a wonderful compilation of answers to general questions people have about cats, and it's stuffed with feline links. For more resources, tap into **Judith Bermans List of Feline WWW Sites** (**http://felinewww.com**)— an ever-growing worldwide directory of feline-related links. **Kitty Sites.com** (**http://www.kittysites.com**) from Mary Zinnecker is another link directory.

CORNELL FELINE HEALTH CENTER
http://web.vet.cornell.edu/Public/FHC/brochure.html

The Cornell Feline Health Center offers client information brochures in general health care, infectious diseases, and medical disorders. Some general care brochures include Choosing and Caring for Your New Cat, Feeding Your Cat, and The Special Needs of the Senior Cat.

CAT-E CORNER
http://www.cat-E-corner.com

A virtual community devoted to cats and their fans, you'll find special features, tips, advice, photos, a discussion forum, and resources.

The makers of Friskies® canned and dry cat food (**http://www.friskies.com**) sponsor a series of Web sites crammed with exceptional feline-related information. Feline Behavior (**http://www.Feline-behavior.com**) is one site. Others include:

- **CHOOSING A CAT**
http://www.Choosing-a-Cat.com

- **FELINE BREEDS**
http://www.felinebreeds.com

- **EVERYTHING YOU EVER WANTED TO KNOW ABOUT CATS**
http://www.Everything-you-ever-wanted-to-know-about-cats.com

- **CARE FOR MY CAT**
http://www.care-for-my-cat.com

- **SPRAYING AND MARKING**
http://www.Spraying-and-marking.com

- **CATS AND DIETS**
http://www.cats-and-diets.com

- **CALM YOUR CAT**
http://www.calm-your-cat.com

CATS FROM ABOUT.COM
http://cats.about.com

Franny Syufy is your guide to cats at About.com. Each week Franny offers new articles and resources, and her vast site brims with a health resource index, feline fun, how-to tips, and information in topics on everything from adopting cats to kitten care and kitty cartoons. Join the active community corner to tap into weekly chats, sign up for a free newsletter, or participate in bulletin board discussions.

THE FELINE INFORMATION PAGE
http://www.best.com/~sirlou/cat.shtml

Learn about cat history, evolution, and nutrition at this illuminating site from Louis E. Kahn. You'll also find lengthy breed descriptions, info on choosing a cat, a species chart, and an ample selection of cat resources.

CATS OF AUSTRALIA
http://hello.to/catsofaustralia

Zoe Berry shares an easy-to-navigate mix of the playful and the informative. The fun includes free cat postcards, cat names, cat quotes, reader-contributed stories, and zodiac info. The informative includes cat care articles, breed descriptions, a list of breeders in Australia, and Vet Talk—offering articles and resources.

CAT FANCIERS
http://www.fanciers.com

This cat community offers extensive cat breed descriptions, a large selection of cat shows, cat clubs and registries, up-to-date veterinary medicine documents and resources, rescue and shelter information, and myriad cat-related links. If you're looking for a breeder, tap into The Fanciers Breeder Referral List which includes over 1,200 Internet-connected breeders of pedigreed cats.

*If you want to discuss cats, joint the Fanciers mailing list, a private, unmoderated list (****http://www.fanciers.com/joining.html***).*

THE CAT CENTER FROM NETPETS
http://www.netpets.org/cats/index.html

Here's a great assortment of cat-related articles and a substantial collection of feline-related links and resources.

PETCAT
http://www.petcat.com

Cat Facts contains all sorts of cat information, a gallery of photos, and cat trivia. The Playground includes lots of fun such as a trivia quiz, free postcards, and a free Paw Pong PC/Mac screensaver you can download. Features includes articles, breed of the month, a vet column, and more. If you register at this site (it's free), you can adopt a virtual cat, get your cat care questions personally answered, and add your personal events to an online calendar that is filled with global cat events and world holidays.

ALL ABOUT CATS
http://allcatz.tripod.com

Visit the advice page for basic cat care information from pros and other cat owners; read cat stories; join a live chat or post a message on the All About Cats message board; view photos; or listen to cat-themed music such as the Pink Panther Theme *or* Eye of the Tiger *(from "Rocky").*

CYBER-CAT
http://www.cyberpet.com/cybercat

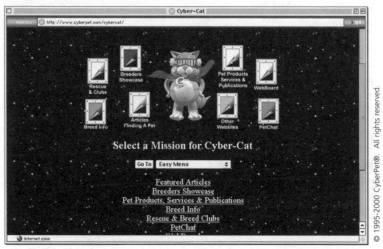

The Mission Impossible theme song greets you at this playful site with serious cat counsel. You'll find numerous articles in a wide variety of topics, a chat room claiming to be the coolest of the Net, a message board, and resources to cat breeds, breeders, rescue organizations, and clubs.

CATS LOVERS CENTRAL AT IVILLAGE.COM
http://www.ivillage.com/pets/cats

Are you looking for insight into your cat's behavior? Ask Pam Johnson-Bennett, a feline behaviorist, your question. Or visit the Think Like A Cat bulletin board to read answers to the questions of others. Cat Lovers Central also includes articles, photos, and various message boards.

CAT CARE FROM THE HUMANE SOCIETY OF THE US
http://www.hsus.org/programs/companion/pet_care/cat_care.html

Outstanding information and recommendations on cat care. Topics include: Be a responsible cat owner; cat care facts; myths about cats; all cats should be indoor cats; cleaning a cat's claws; and more.

MOGGIES HOME OF THE ONLINE CAT GUIDE
http://www.moggies.co.uk

*Moggies is devoted to the health and well-being of kittens and cats everywhere. The **Cat Guide Index** (**http://www.moggies .co.uk/catguide/toc.html**) includes a table of contents to the extensive array of articles included at this site, all designed to increase your cat's enjoyment of its life and your enjoyment of your cat.*

☷ FELINE FUTURE
http://www.felinefuture.com

You'll find a superb detailed reference of the nutritional needs of domestic cats, an introduction on how to prepare a home-made diet for cats, and a marvelous collection of articles on cat care.

CINDY'S CAT PAGES
http://www.cindydrew.com/cats

Cindy's offers engaging cat facts, advice, behavior guidance, a list of common plants dangerous to cats, literature reviews, cat pictures, cat poetry, free graphics, and numerous resources.

T I P

A cat's claws are used for balance and for exercising and stretching the muscles in its legs, back, shoulders, and paws. If you're pondering whether to declaw or not, visit **Educate! Don't Amputate!** (**http://www.lisaviolet.com/cathouse/declaw.html**) to read an assortment of articles on the topic, including a veterinary technician's comprehensive guide to training your cat to scratch appropriately.

Also visit **The Facts About Declawing** (**http://www.maxshouse.com/facts_about_declawing.htm**) and **Stop Your Cat From Scratching Without Declawing** (**http://www.catscratching.com**) for additional guidance.

More free Free Help for Cat Lovers

CHAPTER 12

Cats can dance. Cats can paint. And cats can be trained to use the toilet. No doubt about it, cats are cool. The coolest cats are those well cared for by their owners. This chapter offers an eclectic mix of feline sites—some offering thought-provoking wisdom, others pure entertainment—all designed to help you support and pay homage to your purr-fect pet.

CUTE CATS
http://www.cutecats.com

What else can you find here other than oodles of cute cats? An active discussion board, downloadable adorable cat background images, free cat e-cards, cat clip art, including animations, and plenty of cat resources.

CATS AT SUITE 101
http://www.suite101.com/welcome.cfm/cats

Caroline Anderson is your host to articles, bulletins, and resources for cat fanciers.

 **BRATCATS**
http://www.bratcats.com

From the fanciful—top ten signs your cat has learned your Internet password; why cats are better than people—to the thought-provoking, this site from Maxine Hellman includes an extensive array of feline articles. A bulletin board and extensive links are included.

KITTEN CARE
http://www.kittencare.com

Home to Simba's letters—a collection of questions and answers on a broad range of care, behavior, and health-related issues.

SOME MOORE CATS
http://www.somemoorecats.com

Many cute and cuddly cat photos, several cat-related games, a catcam, a free cat postcard center, and related resources.

> **T I P**
>
> **Can't think of a cat name?** Visit the **Catnames List** (**http://www.microserve.net/~dave/catnames.html**) by Don S. Gladden, modified and maintained by Dave Ratcliffe. This whopper of an alphabetized list includes more than 6,700 names!

CATS 'N KITTENS
http://www.cats.alpha.pl

Agnieszka Radtke of Warsaw, Poland offers a large selection of cat-related articles and resources in topics such as cat humor, facts, superstitions, quotes, breed descriptions, and care. Agnieszka also offers a lovely selection of free cat-related graphics such as backgrounds, borders, images, desktop wallpaper, and icons.

 WORLD OF CATS
http://www.justcatz.com

Visit Catnip Corner for articles on grooming and health issues.

DR. LARRY'S KITTY LITERACY
http://www.drlarrypetvet.com/kitty.html

Where should you go to adopt a new kitten? What do you need to know before you bring a new kitten home? How do you introduce the new kitten to your other animals? Dr. Larry answers these and other questions.

TIP

Can you really train your feline friend to use the toilet? The folks at **How to Toilet Train Your Cat** (**http://www.karawynn.net/mishacat/toilet.shtml**) believe you can. It offers complete, down-to-earth advice and step-by-step instructions, including photos to prove that kitty toilet training is not just a pipe dream. Susan Dennis shares her cat's toilet training adventures in **Toilet Training Cats** (**http://www.susandennis.com/catsquickstart.htm**). If you want to chat with others on how to convince your cat to give up the litter box, you can join Susan's **Toilet Training List** (**http://www.susandennis.com/list.htm**). What the cat does with the toilet seat is another issue.

FROM THE CAT'S POINT OF VIEW
http://www.perfectpaws.com/cpv.html

Read Gwen Bohnenkamp's entertaining and superb book, "From the Cat's Point of View." Topics include aggression, basic training, scratching furniture, territorial behavior problems, and other subjects.

VEGAS THE CAT
http://www.vegasthecat.com

Well-designed and enjoyable, this site features photos and amusing tales of adventures of Vegas, the cat. Cat jokes, quotes, trivia, names, and topnotch resources are included.

WHY CATS PAINT
FROM THE MUSEUM OF NON-PRIMATE ART
http://www.monpa.com/index.html

*Learn about the fascinating world of feline art—including its history, methods for testing feline creative intelligence, feline art links, and other related topics. Think you can recognize a genuine cat painting from a fake? Visit **Dealing with Fake Works** (**http://www.monpa.com/wcp/fakes.html**) and find out. If the thought of cats painting sounds far-fetched, the Museum includes a couple online videos in Quicktime format on "prominent cat artists and their work." Wow, eh?*

CATS WHO QUILT
http://www.catswhoquilt.com

Judy Heim shares stories and resources for cat-loving quilters. Be sure to read the sewing room safety tips to understand the importance of keeping your pins, threads, and sewing notions away from your cats—and dogs.

CAT HOBBYIST
http://www.cathobbyist.com

This information portal for cat lovers includes news, chat room, bulletin boards, links to mailing lists, and other resources.

CLEVER CATS—HOW TO TRICK AND BEHAVIOR TRAIN CATS
http://members.aol.com/goforasail/clevercats.html

Enlightening details as to why cats are not as independent as most people think. Behavior training guidelines and easy tricks you can teach your cat are included.

THE RAGDOLL CONNECTION NETWORK
http://www.ragdoll-cats.com

Calling all Ragdoll cats lovers. Here's where you'll find photos, questions and answers, a bulletin board, and plenty of information about these lovely cats.

GARBO'S WORLD OF CATS FROM MYPETSTOP.COM
http://www.mypetstop.com/usa

Click the Garbo icon for articles in nutrition, ownership, health care, behavior, travel/moving, and other cat-related topics.

PURINA CATS
http://www.purina.com/cats/default.asp

🛒 BONO'S CYBER CATHOUSE
http://www.pro-Bono.net/index.html

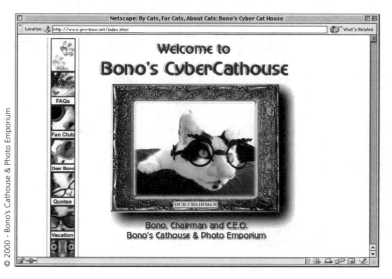

Welcome to
Bono's CyberCathouse

OUR CHAIRMAN

Bono, Chairman and C.E.O.
Bono's Cathouse & Photo Emporium

*Not the vocalist from U2, but the cyber-cat is featured at this high-spirited, frisky site. Join Bono's fan club, learn about his travels, read the clever Cat Users Manual, and send free BonoGram e-postcards to your favorite feline-loving friends (**http://www.pro-bono.net/html/cardrack.html**).*

CATS—MILD TO WILD FROM THE LOS ANGELES NATURAL HISTORY MUSEUM
http://www.lam.mus.ca.us/cats

FOLLOW PFELIX FROM PFIZER
http://www.petnet.com/pfelix

Pfelix is your cyberguide to the fascinating world of cats. Take the cat lifestyle quiz, read health tips for outdoor and indoor cats, and learn about preventable feline diseases.

DANCING WITH CATS
FROM THE MUSEUM OF NON-PRIMATE ART
http://www.monpa.com/dwc/index.html

The question is not whether your cat with dance with you, but if you will dance with your cat. This site includes the history of feline dance, tips, an online exhibit of cat dancing photographs, and more.

free Web Sites of Cat Magazines and E-Zines

Have a favorite cat magazine? Chances are it has a Web site. Wondering about joining a cat club or association? Visit their Web site to see what they offer. Looking for more cat stories, advice, and photos? Read an e-zine, an online magazine with content only available on the Web. This collection of magazines, e-zines, associations, and clubs offer a cornucopia of cat-related guidance and feline fun.

 Free Web Sites of Cat Magazines and E-Zines

CATS & KITTENS MAGAZINE
http://www.catsandkittens.com

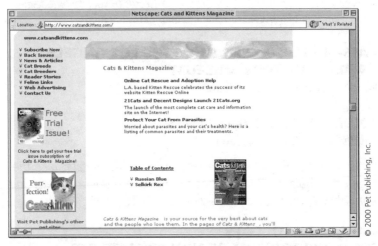

© 2000 Pet Publishing, Inc.

Visit News & Articles for a super selection of features from the print publication. Cat Breeds includes lengthy profiles on several breeds of cats, from the Abyssinian through the Turkish Angora. Cat breeders, reader stories, and related links are also available.

🛒 CATHOUSE & GARDEN
http://www.pro-Bono.net/html/zine.html

This official e-zine of the cathouse lifestyle is a witty, enchanting treat. Learn whether lobster is the perfect party food, read catnip confessions, discover the secret life of cat nappers, and take a peak inside Ms. Ali's special room. Who is Ms. Ali? Tap in and find out.

 ## CAT CAT CAT E-ZINE
http://catcatcat.com

This charming e-zine calls itself a little oasis for cat lovers and friends of the feline creature. It includes news, valuable information on a variety of cat care topics, articles dealing with problem behavior, photos, resources, and a cat chat.

CAT RAGS E-ZINE
http://www.catrags.com

Amusing cat tales are published each Tuesday morning in this cat-oriented, kid- and adult-friendly e-zine. Back issues are available.

FANC-E-MEWS E-ZINE
http://www.cfainc.org/ezine/index.html

Visit this e-zine of The Cat Fanciers Association to read regular columns—including health and cat care topics—feature articles, book reviews, breed spotlight, area cat show information, and pet legislation hot spots around the country.

CATZINE
http://www8.50megs.com/catzine

Sign up to receive CatZine's free newsletter or peruse the site for "news and mews," photos, and other affable feline fun.

CATS MAGAZINE
http://www.catsmag.com

The Web site of this print publication includes features, cat tales, photos, book reviews, a bulletin board, calendar, and other info.

Free Web Sites of Cat Associations and Clubs

CATS UNITED INTERNATIONAL
http://www.catsunited.com

This engaging site includes a terrific section called "Cat Health from A to Z." It includes everything from cat acne and cat allergies to vaccinations and Zoonose Disease. You'll also find a large informative alphabetized list of cat breeds, whopping resources, and links to cat clubs and associations around the world.

ALLEY CAT ALLIES
http://www.alleycat.org

THE INTERNATIONAL CAT ASSOCIATION
http://www.tica.org

Looking for a club for your favorite breed of cat?
Visit **Cat Breeds Clubs** from Netpets
(**http://www.netpets.org/cats/catclub.html**) for an
alphabetized link directory to clubs around the world.

THE CAT FANCIERS ASSOCIATION
http://www.cfainc.org

*This is the world's largest registry of pedigreed cats. The site
details the latest news and includes lavish information on cat
breeds and care.*

THE TRADITIONAL CAT ASSOCIATION
http://www.tcainc.org

THE EDMONTON CAT FANCIERS CLUB
http://www.edmontoncat.ab.ca

THE TRADITIONAL SIAMESE CAT ASSOCIATION U.K.
http://members.tripod.co.uk/TSCA/index.html

THE CAT FANCIERS FEDERATION
http://www.cffinc.org

THE CANADIAN CAT ASSOCIATION
http://www.cca-afc.com

THE AMERICAN ASSOCIATION OF CAT ENTHUSIASTS, INC.
http://www.aaceinc.org

INTERNET CAT CLUB
http://www.netcat.org

SIAMESE INTERNET CAT CLUB
http://www.meezer.com

Tap into this site for photos, history, FAQs, message boards, chat room, breed info, electronic postcards, and links to Siamese Cat rescue organizations.

HAPPY HOUSEHOLD PET CAT CLUB
http://www.best.com/~slewis/HHPCC

Need a place for your cat to play? Visit **Do It Yourself Cat Tree** (**http://amby.com/cat_site/cattree.html**) for complete instructions from Amby Duncan-Carr on building a four-perch cat tree measuring 2' wide, 2' deep, and 4'–6" high.

free Help for Tropical Fish Lovers

When I was a kid, I won a pair of goldfish in a small bowl at a boardwalk game of chance. Unfortunately, they didn't last long. My next pair of goldfish met a similar harsh fate. It wasn't until years later, when I met a man with many aquariums, a man I'd later marry, that I learned goldfish require more than a teeny bowl and fish flakes to live a long life. Today we have a 150-gallon freshwater tank and two 45-gallon saltwater tanks in our home—each a living, evolving work of art. While gazing upon the watery-world is a tranquil treat, problems occur. When they do, we turn to the Web for solutions. Whether you're a new hobbyist seeking general instruction or a consummate aquarist looking for answers to specific questions, there are many Web sites that offer guidance. This chapter contains a collection of large, general sites offering expert advice, stunning photographs, and plenty of inspiration for all levels. Chapter 15 contains more sites. For more resources, visit **Fish Link Central** (**http://www.fishlink central.com**).

JAWS—JUST AQUARIA WEB SITE
http://www.fishgeeks.com

JAWS is dedicated to freshwater, marine, brackish aquaria and their inhabitants, and ponds. Use the drop-down menu to navigate through this extensive site. If you have a question, tap into one of the many message boards.

FISH FROM WALTHAM
http://www.waltham.com/sections/Fish/index.html

This site is bursting with excellent goldfish, marine fish, and tropical freshwater fish information.

AQUAWORLD NETWORK
http://www.aquaworldnet.com

Raffaele Bufo of Italy is a doctor of medicine and a passionate creator of Web sites and graphics for fish lovers. His extensive multi-lingual site includes a cornucopia of resources. Visit Aquaria Info-Cards for information on numerous marine or freshwater species of fish, invertebrates, and plants. Aquaria Veterinary covers a broad range of diseases and therapy. Additionally, this site is a portal to Raffaele's other sites. Two sites bursting with articles, chat rooms, forums, and resources are **Discus Breeders' Web Site** (**http://www.aquaworldnet.com/dbws.shtml**) and The Cichlids' House (**http://www.aquaworldnet.com/tch.shtml**).

THE *.AQUARIA FAQS
http://www.aquaworldnet.com/faq/map.html

An enormous compilation of answers to your general questions taken from the rec-aquaria newsgroup. Topics include your first freshwater aquarium, beginning saltwater aquaria, live plants, disease, algae, snails, other resources, and the FAQ Annex.

⚞ FISHBASE
http://www.fishbase.org

A searchable database on the biology of just about every fish known to science—over 25,000 species. The database is also available on CD-ROM.

🛒 AQUATICS UNLIMITED ONLINE
http://www.bestfish.com

You'll find an extensive collection of articles covering equipment, fish compatibility, maintenance, saltwater, garden ponds, water chemistry, fish health, aquatic plants, and miscellaneous topics.

FINS—THE FISH INFORMATION SERVICE
http://www.actwin.com/fish

Mark Rosenstein's terrific site includes articles, answers to frequently asked questions, an index of marine and freshwater fish species, do-it-yourself plans—including an FAQ on building a fish room, working with acrylic, skimmers, and wet/dry trickle filters—and numerous links to mailing lists, aquarium clubs, national and international societies, and related resources. A chat room is available.

AQUA WEB FISH RESOURCES
http://aquaweb.pair.com

If you have questions about loaches, this is where to find the answers. You'll find news, a loach species index, FAQs, QuickTime loach movies, and resources to loach and other fish-related sites. There are also message boards for loaches, freshwater fish, and marine fish.

AQUARIA CENTRAL—FRESHWATER AND MARINE AQUARIUM FISH
http://www.aquariacentral.com

Discussion boards, chat, aquaria articles, and species profiles of over 500 fish species are featured. Myriad resources and links to other sites are included.

AQUALINK AQUARIA SERVICE
http://www.aqualink.com

David D. Kreg maintains this mammoth resource dedicated to fish-keepers interested in freshwater and marine fish, aquatic plants, goldfish, reef systems, invertebrates, and corals. You'll find loads of articles, an aquaria glossary, disease diagnoser, message boards, clip art, screensavers, and other fish fun.

AQUARIST.NET
http://www.aquarist.net

The goal of Mark Carter's Aquarist.net is to provide a complete guide to every aspect of fishkeeping. You'll find articles on tropical marine fish, coldwater fish, marine invertebrates, aquarium maintenance, bacteria, filtration, lighting, water quality, cause and treatment of disease, conservation issues, and more. Several discussion forums, upcoming events, and related resources are available.

THE KRIB—AQUARIA AND TROPICAL FISH
http://www.thekrib.com

Erik Olson details freshwater aquatic plants and dwarf cichlids, and also includes information on a variety of other subjects, including tank hardware, plumbing and filtration, lighting, and diseases.

*The Aquaria FAQs (**http://faq.thekrib.com**), an outstanding compilation of information taken from the rec-aquaria news-group, is included.*

FISH INDEX.COM
http://www.fishindex.com

© 1997-2000 Fishindex.com

Have a question? Visit one of several very active message boards for answers. Want to learn? Tap into the Aquarium School which offers free Internet classes, including Aquatic Plant 101, Filtration 101, Freshwater Aquariums 100, and Aquarium Myths. Looking for a fish-related store in your area? Try the Store Directory with a nationwide database of fish stores and dealers. Yearning to see Clown Loaches feeding? View an online video. This marvelous site also includes a fascinating selection of articles, fish profiles, and resources.

THE FISHROOM
http://kplace.monrou.com

In 1995, Kevin Carpenter created this interactive discussion area for people interested in aquarium keeping. Complete information on how to connect to any of the many specialty chat rooms, such as reefs, marine breeding, cichlids, and livebearers, is detailed. Additionally, you'll find FAQs for reef keepers and freshwater fish fans, tank pictures, a coral trading board, and other resources.

TROPICA AQUARIUM PLANTS
http://www.tropica.dk

Whether you are a seasoned aquarist or a newcomer, you'll find exceptional guidance on tropical aquarium plants and their care from Tropica, a Danish nursery for aquarium plants. Related articles are included.

EFISH TANK.COM
http://www.eFishTank.com

Looking for an easy way to calculate your tank volume? Salinity? Hardness? You'll find calculators here to help. If you register (it's free), you can also track your fish tank's chemistry online and receive e-mail reminders when it's time to change the water. Related bulletin boards are available.

AQUATIC NET
http://www.aquanet.com

The Aquatic Network provides information about living resources and technology relating to marine and fresh-water environments. Subject areas include aquaculture, conservation, fisheries, limnology, marine science and oceanography, maritime heritage, ocean engineering, and seafood.

WETWEBMEDIA.COM
http://www.wetwebmedia.com

What causes bloated gut in a trigger fish? How can you get your yellow tang to eat a well-balanced diet? Is there any way to control red slime? Author Robert Fenner answers these and other questions, or e-mail him your question. This vast resource features articles and FAQs in marine, freshwater, aquarium plants, ponds, brackish systems, and aquatics business topics.

Free downloadable desktop calendars featuring a beautiful aquatic image are available.

More **free** Help for Tropical Fish Lovers

Owning an aquarium of fish is generally easier to maintain than most pets. You don't need to walk 'em, will never have to clean their unwanted droppings off the floor, and they won't trigger an allergic reaction in your guests. Even so, creating a thriving aquarium takes some work and patience. Water can get cloudy; too much algae can grow; disease can occur; some fish are more aggressive than others—you don't, for example, want to mix fin-nipping tiger barbs in a tank filled with slow-moving fancy-tailed guppies. To emphasize the pleasures and avoid the hazards, tap into this collection of sites where you'll find fish-loving enthusiasts eager to share their wisdom with you. A collection of magazine sites is included.

Free Help for Freshwater Fish Lovers

FRESHWATER AQUARIUMS AT ABOUT.COM
http://freshaquarium.about.com

Ever wonder what is the most popular aquarium fish? If you guessed goldfish, you're right. Popular Aquarium Fish is just one of the many feature articles from Shirley Sharpe, the freshwater aquariums guide at About.com. You'll also find aquarium set-up guides, a freshwater fish chat, bulletin boards, fish photos, extensive resources, and a free newsletter you can sign up for.

FRESHWATER FISH FAQS
http://dafishdude.cjb.net

No matter your level of experience, this site has plenty to offer. Topics include setting up your tank; algae info, water, plants, and tank maintenance; selecting, adding, feeding, breeding, and moving your fish; dealing with sick fish—and more.

WRR AQUATECH
http://www.wrraquatech.com

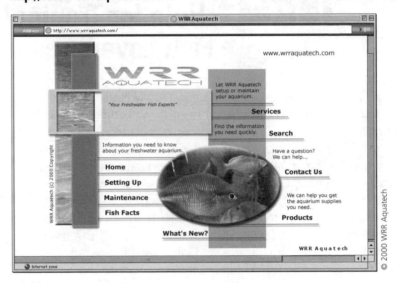

This attractive and easy-to-navigate site includes marvelous information on setting up and maintaining a freshwater aquarium. Visit Fish Facts for the lowdown on fish types, filtration, algae, water conditions, medicines, diseases, plants, fish food, tips from the experts, and more. Have a question regarding any of the site's topics? Free advice is just an e-mail away.

FISHY WEB
http://fishyweb.tripod.com

Fishy Web includes tutorials, fish gallery, message board, and related info—all geared toward the freshwater aquarium hobbyist.

TROPICAL FISH CENTRE
http://www.tropicalfishcentre.co.uk

Do you want to know about filtration and aeration? Do you care about water changes or the nitrogen cycle? Do you know how to buy the correct fish for your tank? Should you mix goldfish with tetras? These questions and many others are answered at this vast site that includes information on setting up an aquarium, choosing your fish, aquatic plants, fish diseases, species guide, feeding and diet, a message board, and more.

FRESHWATER INFORMATION SERVICE HOMEPAGE (FISH)
http://www.worldzone.net/family/aquaria

Great beginner information, fish profiles, and an active message board are some of the topics on this growing site.

CICHLID RESEARCH HOME PAGE
http://cichlidresearch.com

Ron Coleman, Ph.D., offers both the scientific researcher and the hobbyist a wealth of cichlid fish information.

AQUA ZONE
http://www.digicron.com/AquaZone

The freshwater hobbyist will enjoy the photo gallery and large library of articles covering topics such as algae eaters, tetras, snails in your aquarium, lighting techniques, and travel and your aquarium. Sign up for a free newsletter or join the freshwater discussion group. Additional resources are included.

THE GOLDFISH TANK
http://www.koivet.com/goldinfo

Dr. Erik Johnson explains goldfish care and treatment of disorders.

Nothing is more pleasant for a fish lover than spending an afternoon at an aquarium. In addition to general information, these favorite aquariums feature extras on their sites such as fish cams, learning centers, virtual tours, and related resources.

- **MONTEREY BAY AQUARIUM, MONTEREY, CA**
http://www.mbayaq.org

- **BIRCH AQUARIUM AT SCRIPPS INSTITUTE OF OCEANOGRAPHY IN LA JOLLA, CA**
http://www.aquarium.ucsd.edu

- **AK-SAR-BEN AQUARIUM, NE**
http://ngp.ngpc.state.ne.us/parks/aquarium.html

- **NEW ENGLAND AQUARIUM, BOSTON, MA**
http://www.neaq.org

- **OREGON COAST AQUARIUM, NEWPORT, OR**
http://www.aquarium.org

- **TENNESSEE AQUARIUM, CHATTANOOGA, TN**
http://www.tennis.org

- **THE SEATTLE AQUARIUM, SEATTLE, WA**
http://www.seattleaquarium.org

- **NEW JERSEY STATE AQUARIUM, NJ**
http://www.njaquarium.org

- **THE NATIONAL AQUARIUM IN BALTIMORE, MD**
http://www.aqua.org

- **VANCOUVER AQUARIUM MARINE SCIENCE CENTRE, VANCOUVER, BC**
http://www.vancouver-aquarium.org

- **SYDNEY AQUARIUM, SYDNEY, NSW, AUSTRALIA**
http://www.sydneyaquarium.com.au

Free Help
for the Saltwater Fish Lovers

SALTWATER AQUARIUMS FROM ABOUT.COM
http://saltaquarium.about.com

Stan and Debbie Hauter are your witty and wise hosts to saltwater aquariums at About.com. You'll find everything from algae control to tank photos, extensive growing resources about the identification, characteristics, and dietary needs of various saltwater fish and invertebrates; fish store and online supplier reviews; feature articles, bulletin board and chat sessions; and a free newsletter that you can subscribe to.

THE SALTWATER AQUARIUM GUIDE
http://www.marineaquarium.org

This full-featured site includes everything you need to know about setting up a saltwater aquarium, controlling algae, the nitrogen cycles, fish compatibility, diet and feeding, diseases and treatment, fish families—and more. Or use the site's search engine to help you find exactly what you're looking for. You can also subscribe to a free newsletter and join the active message boards.

FISH DOMAIN
http://www.fishdomain.com

Claiming to be the definitive source for the saltwater aquarium enthusiast, this site is loaded with articles, a how-to series, FAQs, species and invertebrates guides, tank, lighting, and filtration info, and an active message board.

LIVADASLAND MARINE FISH—THE MARINE AQUARIUM HOBBYIST WEB SITE
http://www.marineaquarium.com

Visit the Info Center for start up, filtration, fish selection, fish feeding, first aid, and the green room, where you can learn how to combat unwanted algae growth. Send a free marine post card to your friends or family. Visit the message center or a join a chat.

THREE STEPS TO A REEF AQUARIUM
http://www.mcs.net/~rogers/frame.html

If you're willing to invest the time and money, the beauty of a Reef-Aquarium can be achieved. Matthew Rogers details in three steps what you need to know.

REEFKEEPERS FAQS
http://www.actwin.com/fish/reefkeepers/index.html

An exceptional compilation of information derived from the UseNet *.aquaria groups.

 # Free Web Sites of Freshwater and Marine Fish Magazines

AQUAWORLD MAGAZINE—THE AQUARIUM WORLD MAGAZINE
http://www.aquaworldnet.com/awmag.shtml

This multi-lingual e-zine includes articles by authors from around the world, stunning photographs, and a chat room. Back issues are available.

PRACTICAL FISHKEEPING
http://www.aquarist.net/pfk/index1.htm

FISH TALK WITH UNCLE BILL
http://www.fishtalk.com

 ## FISHZINE
http://www.fishzine.com

AQUARIUM MAGAZINE
www.aquarium.net

 ## AQUARIUM FISH
http://www.animalnetwork.com/fish/default.asp

FRESHWATER AND MARINE AQUARIUM
http://www.mag-web.com/fama

TROPICAL FISH HOBBYIST
http://www.tfh.com

AQUACULTURE MAGAZINE
http://www.aquaculturemag.com

TIP

If you're thinking about building a fish pond, visit **"Building A Pond" by Guy Lovren** (**http://www.exit109.com/~gosta/pond.sht**) where you'll find Guy's extensive online book complete with illustrations. He offers no-nonsense advice on pond building, installing a filtration system pump, creating waterfalls, and other advice.

Other helpful sites include **The Pond Pages** (**http://www.thepondpages.com**), Greg's Pond and Koi Farm (**http://www.geocities.com/bickal2000/pond.htm**), Pete's Pond Page (**http://reality.sgi.com/peteo**), and the Half-Barrel Pond Page (**http://www.jeffcook.com/ hbpond.html**) where Jeff Cook discusses all aspects of building a half-barrel pond, including resources.

free Help for Bird Lovers

I'm enamoured with Andy, my dad's cockatiel. Andy is only slightly larger than my hand, but he whistles in a high octave tunes like *The Sailor's Hornpipe* and *The Old Waterhole* with a zestful clarity and unabashed pride far greater than his size. When Andy is in a particularly spirited mood, he'll punctuate his tunes with a slight vibrato. He also sweetly speaks little phrases such as "night-night," "whatcha doing," and "gimmekiss" while perched in his cage or on my dad's shoulder. For many people, the company of a beautiful bird is an attractive alternative to other pets. Whether you own a single cockatiel or an aviary full of parrots, the sites in this chapter can help you better understand and care for your bird. If you are considering the addition of a feathered-friend to your dwelling, these sites will help you determine the right bird for your lifestyle. For those fascinated by observing winged creatures, bird-watching sites are also included.

Free Advice for Pet Bird Lovers

BIRDS AT ABOUT.COM
http://birds.about.com

Vera Appleyard hosts this marvelous bird site where you'll find extensive feature articles, detailed species profiles, a 24-hour live chat room, bulletin board, a free weekly newsletter you can subscribe to, and extensive resources.

ANSWERS ABOUT BIRDS FROM PETSMART.COM
http://www.petsmart.com/bird/answers

Bird care guides are available for a large assortment of breeds. Visit FAQs for answers to questions such as why is my bird screaming. A number of articles on feeding and health, housing, and other topics are included.

FEATHER JUNCTION AVIARY
http://members.tripod.com/~Feather_Junction/junction.html

You'll find plenty of useful articles and numerous resources for exotic bird lovers.

PET BIRD BY UP AT SIX AVIARIES
http://www.upatsix.com

Myriad avian articles, associations, suppliers, mailing lists, online chat groups and message boards, and more from Up at Six Aviaries. Favorite behavior articles by Liz Wilson include **Parrot Behavioral Myths and Misinformation (http://www3.upatsix.com/liz/ articles/ myths.html)***, Is It True You Can't Tell When a Bird is Sick? (***http://www3.upatsix.com/ liz/articles/sick.html***), and Biting Parrots—Why They Do It and How To Control It (***http://www3.upatsix.com/liz/articles/biting.html***). Be sure to visit* **Pet Bird FAQ (http://www.upatsix.com/faq/index.html)***, for an extensive searchable collection of information gathered by Jodi L. Giannini. Species-specific FAQs cover everything from Amazons, budgerigars, canaries, and cockatiels to quaker parakeets and toucans.*

HOTSPOT FOR BIRDS
http://www.multiscope.com/hotspot

© 2000 HotSpot for Birds

Tap into the reference section for a multitude of articles on keeping your birds safe and healthy.

BIRD HOBBYIST
http://www.birdhobbyist.com

This information portal for the avian enthusiast includes several active bulletin boards, a chat room, events and organizations, and plenty of resources.

WALTHAM—BIRDS
http://www.waltham.com/sections/Birds/index.html

This site highlights the choosing, feeding, training, and breeding of birds. Photography tips, FAQs, and wild bird info are also included.

BIRDS N WAY—
GUIDE TO PARROTS AND EXOTIC PET BIRDS
http://www.birdsnways.com

Well-organized and jam-packed with parrot and exotic bird information, you'll find a library of articles, FAQs, and extensive resources. Visit Chit Chat and Sharing for forums, chat rooms, and mailing list subscription information. Some of the many useful sites include **Birds N Way Recipe Exchange (http://www.birds nways.com/birds/recipes.htm)**, Exotic Bird Associations and Bird Clubs **(http://www.birdsnways.com/birds/assoc.htm)**, and Avian Nutrition **(http://www.RCreation.com/aprvet_pg.html)**.

THE PET BIRD PAGE
http://www.petbirdpage.com

This site details many different bird breeds.

CAGEBIRD.COM
http://www.cagebird.com

Visit the Cagebird cam to view live birds. Other info includes breeders, a bird show calendar, clubs, photos, chat sites, mailing list resources, and related sites.

THE AUSTRALIAN BIRDMAN
http://birdman.humbled.com

This cheery Aussie "birdman" shares many informative articles under general, breeding, diet, health, and species-specific topics. Related resources are included.

CARING FOR YOUR NEW BIRD, BY KATHY JOHNSON
http://www.ddc.com/~kjohnson/birdcare.htm

CARING FOR YOUR PET BIRD
http://www.healthypet.com/Library/prevent-18.html

BIRD CARE FROM VETNET
http://home.vet.net/index_avian.htm

VetNet, the veterinary Internet hub, provides abundant avian care sheets to several species including African Grey, Amazons, Budgies, Canaries, Cockatiels, Cockatoos, Conures, and others.

Free Guidance for Specific Bird Species

TOOLADY.COM— PARROT, MACAW, COCKATOO AND EXOTIC BIRD RESOURCES
http://www.toolady.com

PARROT LINK UK
http://www.parrot-link.co.uk

PARROT TALK CONNECTION
http://www.ParrotTalk.com

A PLACE FOR CANARIES
http://www.robirda.com

THE PARROT HOUSE
http://www.parrothouse.com

This prodigious site is crammed with excellent articles on avian nutrition and behavior. Be sure to visit the Recipe page (**http://www.parrothouse. com/recipes.html**) for a heap of recipes your birds will love.

THOSE MAJESTIC MACAWS
http://www.exoticbird.com

Barry Thaxton details the flamboyant and captivating macaws, including a compendium of the species, numerous articles, health and care tips, recipes, FAQs, related resources, and other advice.

THE VIRTUAL PARROT
http://www.realmacaw.com

Home to the Real Macaw Parrot Club, whose purpose is to educate and learn about the owning of and caring for all types of parrots. In addition to learning about the Club, you'll find a wonderful selection of articles covering basic bird care, bird buying, and much more. Oodles of resources are included.

HUMMINGBIRDS.NET
http://www.hummingbirds.net

Lanny Chambers offers a splendid source of information on attracting, watching, feeding, and studying North American hummingbirds.

FINCHWORLD
http://www.finchworld.com

This premier source for finch information from Rick Fulmer includes a search engine, information, articles, and resources about favorite finches, such as the Zebra Finch and Society Finch, and including the Lady Gouldian, the Red Cheek Cordon Bleus, the Cut-throat Finch, the Pin-tailed Whydah, Violet-earred Waxbill, and several others. Additional articles and resources are available on health and housing needs topics, and directories for finch lovers and breeders are available.

**T
I
P**

Looking for others to talk to about birds? Tap into Electronic Magazines (**http://members.tripod.com/~ Feather_Junction/ezines.html**) from Feather Junction for an assortment of bird mailing lists with subscription information.

Also visit **Chat Rooms, Mailing Lists, Forums, and Advice** (**http://www.realmacaw.com/pages/chats.html**) for a sizeable resource list with links, courtesy of The Real Macaw Parrot Club. For more information on mailing lists, chat rooms, and forums, see Chapter 3.

Free Advice for Wild Bird Lovers

BACKYARD BIRDING
http://www.bcpl.net/~tross/by/backyard.html

The Baltimore Bird Club details how and what to feed birds, which shrubs and flowers to plant in order to attract birds, and related wisdom. There are also yardlists and journals from backyard birders and links to related sites of interest.

BUILDING A BASIC BIRDBOX
http://home.pacifier.com/~mpatters/bird/nestbox.html

WILD BIRD CENTER OF WALNUT CREEK
http://www.birdware.com

Visit Backyard Birding Tips for articles on the feeding preferences of wild birds, an overview of wild bird feeding, how to create a landscape desirable to birds, and other advice.

BIRD ON! FROM BIRDCARE.COM
http://www.birdcare.com/birdon

This leading news, information, and reference site is dedicated to everyone who is aware of the wild birds around them. It includes a searchable dictionary of bird-watching terminology, and a searchable Encyclopaedia of Birdcare.

OPTICS FOR BIRDING
http://www.optics4birding.com

Edmund R. Matthews educates readers on binoculars and telescopes. You'll find reviews, FAQs, manufacturer contacts, resources, and related advice.

OFFICE OF MIGRATORY BIRD MANAGEMENT
http://migratorybirds.fws.gov

Here are lengthy online brochures from the U.S. Fish and Wildlife Service on backyard bird feeding, backyard bird problems, attracting birds, homes for birds, and migratory songbird conservation.

BIRDING HOTSPOTS AROUND THE WORLD
http://www.camacdonald.com/birding/birding.htm

This walloping site contains information on birding in 200 countries, 10 provinces and 3 territories of Canada, and all 50 U.S. states and Washington, D.C. Personal site guides and a gallery of gorgeous bird photographs are included.

> **TIP**
>
> **Send a virtual pet** greeting to the favorite people in your life by visiting these sites: **Virtual Pets Greeting Cards** (**http://www.123greetings.com/pets**), **Kritter Cards** (**http://www.krittercards.com**), **PuppyGram** (**http://www.petmarket.com/html/dcardshop.html**), and **Action Cat** (**http://www.actioncat.com**).

free Web Sites of Bird Magazines, Associations and Societies

There are many bird magazines, associations, and societies offering Web sites that celebrate the fascinating, often flamboyant and colorful winged creatures known as birds. Their sites are rich with articles, gorgeous photographs, and related resources. This is a collection of some favorites.

 *Free Advice from Bird Magazines*

BIRD TIMES MAGAZINE
http://www.birdtimes.com

Bird Times Magazines covers all types of cage birds, including parrots, canaries, finches, budgerigars, cockatiels, pigeons, and doves. The site includes breed profiles, news and articles from the print publication, reader stories, resources, and more.

WINGED WISDOM
http://www.wingedwisdom.com

COCKATIEL AND PARAKEET WORLD
http://www.seacoastpub.com/cpw_mag.html

FINCH AND CANARY WORLD
http://www.seacoastpub.com/fcw_mag.html

THE PET BIRD REPORT
http://www.petbirdreport.com

BIRD BREEDER
http://www.birdbreeder.com

PARROTS MAGAZINE
http://www.parrotmag.com

INTERBIRDNET
http://www.birder.co.uk

PETERSON BIRDWATCHER DIGEST
http://www.petersononline.com/birds/bwd

ORIGINAL FLYING MACHINE
http://www.originalflyingmachine.com

LEXICON OF PARROTS
http://www.arndt-verlag.com

Free Web Sites
of Bird Associations and Societies

🛒 NATIONAL AUDUBON ASSOCIATION ONLINE
http://www.audubon.org

BIRDNET
http://www.nmnh.si.edu/BIRDNET/index.html

NORTH AMERICAN COCKATIEL SOCIETY
http://www.cockatiel.org

*Visit Cockatiel Care Tips for FAQs, breeding information, recipes, and more.
This site also includes extensive resources, member sites, and an excellent
collection of articles. Some favorites include:*

- **AVIAN NUTRITION, BY CYNTHIA L. KIESEWETTER**
http://www.cockatiel.org/articles/nutrition.html

- **BIRD FIRST AID, BY TERESA LINTON**
http://www.cockatiel.org/articles/firstaid.html

- **ESTABLISHING YOURSELF AS TOP BIRD,
BY LYNN TRAYLOR**
http://www.cockatiel.org/articles/establishing.html

THE AUSTRALIAN NATIONAL COCKATIEL SOCIETY
http://www.bit.net.au/~ancs

In addition to learning about the Society, be sure to tap into the article index for features such as aviary set-up and compatible birds, caged birds and diet, home safety for pet birds, and others.

PARROT SOCIETY OF AUSTRALIA, INC.
http://parrotsociety.org.au

AFRICAN PARROT SOCIETY
http://www.wingscc.com/aps

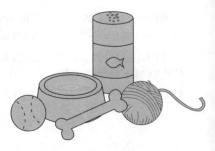 THE AMERICAN COCKATIEL SOCIETY
http://www.acstiels.com

THE NATIONAL COCKATIEL SOCIETY
http://www.cockatiels.org

AMERICAN BIRDING ASSOCIATION
http://www.americanbirding.org

The American Birding Association is North America's largest membership organization for active birders, and its mega-site offers a wonderful resource for all levels—from those just starting out through the skilled field birder. You'll find many inspiring and informative articles and plenty of advice. You'll also find an events calendar, conservation info, a rare bird alert, and more. Some particularly useful sites include:

- **THE BIRDING GOURMET:**
  GREAT RESTAURANTS NEAR AMERICA'S
  BIRDING HOTSPOTS
  http://americanbirding.org/resources/resgourm.htm

- **BIRDING NEWSGROUPS AND MAILING LISTS**
  http://americanbirding.org/abalinks/linkspage5.htm

- **STATE CHAT GROUPS AND MAILING LISTS**
  http://americanbirding.org/resources/reschat.htm

free Help for Horse Lovers

When you think of horses, do you imagine swashbuckling adventurers galloping to new frontiers? Romantic rides into the sunset? Or, do you simply marvel at the glory and splendor of the mighty hoofed animal? Whether you are a new equine devotee or an accomplished rider, the sites in this chapter will educate and enchant. For additional horse-related Web sites, tap into these directories: Hay.Net (**http://www.haynet.net**), Equiworld Horse Links (**http://www.equiworld.net/horselinks**), and NetVet—Horses (**http://netvet.wustl.edu/horses.htm**).

HORSE WEB
http://www.horseweb.com

In addition to finding "hot off the press" new releases, this site is packed with equine-related links and resources. To learn when new material is added, sign up for a free e-mail link digest newsletter.

HORSE COUNTRY
http://www.horse-country.com

*Here's a place you'll return to again and again. Horse Country features a wonderful compilation of articles and resources for all equine enthusiasts—everything from horse-related art and history to a collection of horse-treat recipes. Younger riders will enjoy tapping into the Junior Riders Journal, a place to discuss horse and equestrian concerns, and Gymkhana Interactive for a marvelous selection of quizzes, puzzles, and coloring pages that teach through horse-related fun. If you're looking for a pen-pal who shares your love of horses, visit the Pen Pals page for world-wide listings. You'll also find rec.equestrain FAQs (**http://www.horse-country.com/faqs/index.html**), an encyclopedic collection of answers and resources compiled from the rec.equestrain Usenet newsgroup.*

HORSES AT ABOUT.COM
http://horses.about.com

Jayne Pedigo is your host to extensive articles, resources, an equine glossary, discussion boards, a live chat—and more. If you're a novice, be sure to read the "Beginner's Guide to Horses," which includes information on riding lessons and caring for horses. A free newsletter is available.

HORSE TALK—WORLD EQUESTRIAN NEWS
http://www.horsetalk.co.nz

Can aromatherapy help you and your horse before a dressage competition? Read "Competition Scents for Horse and Rider," one of the many featured articles, to find out. International news, health updates, horse health questions and answers, discussion boards, and live chats are included in this vast site.

HORSE FUN
http://horsefun.com

Did you know that horses often stand tail to tail to protect each other from annoying flies by swishing their tails? Learn this and other horse facts by tapping into this friendly site. You'll also find information on correcting problems such as a horse running when he sees you coming, bucking horses, and handling a horse that's about to roll. Information about "The Horselover's Club for Kids" (yearly fee required) is included.

THE HORSE PAGES
http://www.maroon.com/horses

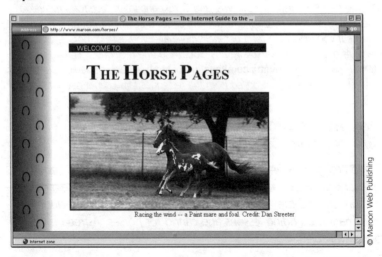

This guide to the world of horses includes information on more than 75 breeds and resources to horse services, supplies, equipment, and publications.

CLASSICAL DRESSAGE
http://www.classicaldressage.com

Dedicated to the art of classical dressage, you'll find a question-and-answer forum, a critique-and-compare forum, a free newsletter and discussion list, articles, photos, and resources.

AMERICA'S HORSE SOURCE
http://www.americashorsesource.com

Training tips, ask-the-vet questions and answers, veterinarian articles, horse stories, horse clubs, breeds, and many other related topics are offered at this comprehensive site.

AMERICA'S QUARTER HORSE PAGE
http://www.quarterh.com

Read about the latest news, events, people, and horses in the Quarter Horse industry. Visit the health page for extensive articles such as causes and cures for colic abdominal pain, a first aid kit for your horse, treating horse influenza, combating cold weather stress, and other topics.

THE SADDLEBRED INFORMATION SOURCE
http://www.trot.org

A portal to the latest news, industry organizations, events, and Saddlebred resources, this site also includes feature articles—such as the history of the American Saddlebred—a message board, and chat room.

THE ARABIAN HORSE NETWORK
http://www.arabhorse.com

APPALOOSA HORSE CLUB
http://www.appaloosa.com

Free Web Sites of Horse Societies, Associations, and Magazines

AMERICAN ASSOCIATION FOR HORSEMANSHIP SAFETY
http://www.law.utexas.edu/dawson/index.htm

Exceptional info on horsemanship safety and legal liability.

AMERICAN QUARTER HORSE ASSOCIATION
http://www.aqha.org

AMERICAN CONNEMARA PONY SOCIETY
http://www.nas.com/acps

AMERICAN PAINT SHOW-HORSE ASSOCIATION
http://www.apha.com

AMERICAN MINIATURE HORSE ASSOCIATION
http://www.minihorses.com

AMERICAN SADDLEBRED HORSE ASSOC. ONLINE
http://saddlebred.com

BRIDLE UP MAGAZINE
http://www.Bridleup.com

HORSE MANIA—A FREE ONLINE NEWSLETTER
http://www.angelfire.com/id/horsemania

HIGHLAND PONY GAZETTE
http://www.highland-pony.demon.co.uk

EQUESTRIENNE.COM
http://equestrienne.com

ARABIAN HORSE WORLD ONLINE
http://www.ahwmagazine.com

PERFORMANCE HORSE MAGAZINE ONLINE
http://www.performancehorse.com

free Help for Exotic Pet Lovers

The term "exotic pets" covers a broad range of small mammals, reptiles, amphibians—even insects. According to the 1999/2000 APPMA National Pet Owners Survey, there are over 4,000,000 households that own a small animal—with rabbits, hamsters, guinea pigs, and gerbils heading the popularity list—and over 2,710,000 households that own snakes, lizards, and other reptiles. While it's a safe assumption that your hamster will remain in its cage and your frogs will not be too demanding, the frisky and energetic ferret is known to get into everything. In other words, some exotics require a greater commitment of time and energy than others. The sites in this chapter will introduce you to the world of exotics, their care, the time commitment the various species require, and whether owning one or more is right for you and your family. Be sure to visit the big sites in Chapter 2 for additional guidance.

Free Advice From Large Web Sites

EXOTIC PET CARE FROM VETNET
http://www.veterinarylibrary.com/main_exoticcare.htm

This online educational center offers care articles for hedgehogs, ferrets, guinea pigs, box turtles, rabbits, and sugar gliders.

OTHER ANIMAL CARE
FROM HUMANE SOCIETY OF THE U.S.
http://www.hsus.org/programs/companion/pet_care/other_
  care.html

Rabbit, guinea pig, ferret, and hamster care guidance.

EXOTIC PET REVIEW
http://homearts.com/depts/pastime/exoticf1.htm

Learn about or discuss exotics such as flying squirrels, sugar gliders, ferrets, prairie dogs, and hedgehogs.

EXOTIC PETS AT ABOUT.COM
http://exoticpets.about.com

Thinking of adding a playful marsupial to your home? Read Housing Sugar Gliders, one of several feature articles by Lianne McLeod, your About.com exotic pets host. Lianne covers the gamut of exotics—everything from amphibians and big cats to wolfdogs and rare species. You'll find a photo gallery, guidance on selecting an exotic pet, a chat room, bulletin boards, a free newsletter, and numerous resources. If your pet is an escape artist, you'll also find tips on how to find him.

More
Free Advice

TORTOISE TRUST
http://www.tortoisetrust.org

The world's largest tortoise and turtle organization shares numerous care sheets, articles, and resources.

TURTLE TIMES
http://www.turtletimes.com

Tap into this search engine to locate turtle-related sites.

HERP (REPTILE) CARE INFORMATION
http://www.sonic.net/~melissk

Melissa Kaplan offers a broad range of comprehensive information on the care, behavior, and breeding of herps. You'll find articles for amphibians, iguanas, invertebrates, lizards, crocodilians, and snakes.

 ## THE REPTILE SHACK
http://www.reptileshack.com

Care sheets for geckos, iguanas, lizards and other reptiles. A help forum and live chat are available.

COMPLETE HAMSTER SITE
http://www.hamsters.co.uk

This ultimate hamster resource explains what you need to know about buying, caring for, and breeding hamsters. You'll find answers to frequently asked questions, an e-mail group to join, a live chat, bulletin boards, hamster club info, and resources.

THE ALT.PETS.HAMPSTERS FAQ
http://www.ggower.com/hamsters/faq.htm

HOUSE RABBIT SOCIETY
http://www.rabbit.org

This national, nonprofit animal welfare organization shares an extensive collection of information on rabbit care.

FERRET CENTRAL
http://www.ferretcentral.org

Exhaustive links to ferret information, including clubs and shelters, health care, references, and directories.

CAVIES GALORE—GUINEA PIGS
http://www.caviesgalore.com

How many cavies should you own? How can you prevent your cavy from getting sick? What type of diet is best? Tap in and find out this and other information. You'll also find active bulletin boards and a chat room.

GERBILS

http://www.gerbils.org

Here's a great place to learn how to care for these lovable rodents.

THE GERBILARIUM
http://members.tripod.com/gerbilarium

Gerbil e-cards, stories, articles, and other fun. Great resources, too.

THE BUNNY BUNCH
http://www.thebunnybunch.org

This bunny rescue organization explains why buying your child a bunny as an Easter present may not be a good idea. Head to Bunny Basics for an assortment of bunny care tips.

RABBITS ONLINE
http://home.att.net/~junyuan

The primary focus is teaching rabbit owners and breeders how to take care of their bunnies. Subscription info for three different rabbit-related e-mail groups is available.

PIGS 4 EVER
http://www.pigs4ever.com

Calling all pig lovers! Read FAQs, piggy stories, and poetry. Learn about upcoming pig events, rescue centers, and organizations. Plenty of pig resources, too.

free Web Sites of Pet-Related TV Shows and Radio Shows

Several pet and animal TV shows host marvelous Web sites offering episode information, show schedules, inspiring photos and stories—even a place to converse with other fans. You can also listen to radio shows on the Net—many of them live. The second half of this chapter tells you how to find pet- and animal-related radio shows and how to set up your browser to listen.

Web Site of Pet TV Shows on Discovery's Animal Planet

Start at **Animal Planet's** main page (**http://www.animal.discovery .com**) to read an ever-changing selection of features or to join in forums. Then head to the page for your favorite pet or animal shows. Use the Search feature if you can't find it. Most of the show pages include special features, video clips, fan forums, and other information. You'll also find directories of episodes.

ANIMAL PLANET'S PET TV SHOWS
http://www.animal.discovery.com/yelpline/pet_shows.html

A directory of popular shows such as Pet Project, Petsburgh USA, Breed All About It, *and* Good Dog U.
Here are some additional Animal Planet favorites:

THE CROCODILE HUNTER
http://animal.discovery.com/crochunter/crochunter.html

THE PLANET'S FUNNIEST ANIMALS
http://animal.discovery.com/tunein/funniest/funniest.html

JUDGE WAPNER'S ANIMAL COURT
http://animal.discovery.com/animalpages/wapner/wapner.html

EMERGENCY VETS
http://animal.discovery.com/animalpages/e-vets/e-vets.html

Pet TV Shows on PBS

Public Television (**http://www.pbs.org**) hosts several marvelous TV shows—and a great Web site. Some favorite shows include:

WOOF!—IT'S A DOG'S LIFE
http://www.pbs.org/wgbh/woof/home.html

ANIMAL ATTRACTIONS— AMAZING TALES FROM THE SAN DIEGO ZOO
http://www.pbs.org/wnet/nature/attractions/html/home.html

NOVA—ANIMAL HOSPITAL
http://www.pbs.org/wgbh/nova/vets/index.html

PBS BIRDWATCH
http://www.pbs.org/birdwatch

WILD HORSES, AN AMERICAN ROMANCE
http://www.pbs.org/wildhorses/wildintro.html

Listen to Pet Radio Shows— Live on the Web!

Wish you could listen to *Talking Pets*, despite the fact that it's not broadcast in your community? Listen to it on the Web. A growing number of Web-cast mega-sites like **Yahoo! Broadcast** (**http://www.broadcast.com**) broadcast radio shows—and some TV shows too. Some shows are aired live. But some you can listen to at any time of the day.

Here's how it works: You install one of the free browser plug-ins that plays audio and video—RealPlayer from RealNetworks, Windows Media Player from Microsoft, or Quicktime from Apple. You tap into a broadcasting Web site like Yahoo! Broadcast. Then click on the broadcast link for the show you wish to listen to or see and—voila!—the show pops up on your screen and plays through your computer's speaker.

Where to Find Live Web Broadcasts of Radio Shows for Pet and Animal Lovers

Tap into Pet Talk America (**http://www.pettalk.com**), *hosted by Bob Vella, and listen to live broadcasts. Or visit the archive to listen to a particular show. You'll also find a 24/7 chat room, answers to general pet questions, resources, and more.*

What You Need:

- A 486 DX or faster PC, or a Power Macintosh with System 8.1 or later.
- A sound card and speakers.
- A reasonably good connection to the Net, at speeds of 28.8K, 56K, or faster. Obviously, a faster connection is better.
- An up-to-date Web browser. Head to the Web site of **Netscape** (**http://www.netscape.com**) or Microsoft (**http://www.microsoft.com**) and download the newest version of the one you use. You'll need a browser that supports Java and JavaScript. Versions of Internet Explorer prior to 5 are unable to play RealAudio files through certain dynamic links, such as an .asp script.
- The free browser plug-in. For RealPlayer, visit **RealNetworks** (**http://www.real.com**) and look for the RealPlayer 8 Basic link near the bottom of the page. For Windows Media Player, go to the **Windows Media Download Center** (**http://www.microsoft.com/ windows/windowsmedia/en/download/default.asp**). For QuickTime go to **Apple's QuickTime Page** (**http://www.apple.com/quicktime**) and click the download link. All plug-ins work with Netscape and Internet Explorer browsers.

YAHOO! BROADCAST
http://www.broadcast.com

YAHOO! BROADCAST—LIVING PETS
http://www.broadcast.com/Home_and_Living/Pets

Information and links to radio shows discussing pets that week.

THE PET FILES RADIO SHOW
http://www.thepetproject.com/thepetfiles.html

Tips for Getting Good Sound and Pictures

• Whether you use RealPlayer or Windows Media Player, keep your multimedia plug-in current by downloading new versions from the makers' Web sites as needed. This will help ensure good sound and video quality.

• Keep your computer's audio and video drivers current by occasionally visiting the Web site of your PC's maker and checking for any driver updates. Out-of-date audio drivers sometimes choke on compressed audio streams from broadcast Web sites.

• Clean out your browser's disk and memory caches regularly to keep audio and video error messages at bay. For instance, if your multimedia player displays an "error 14" message, it's usually due to a loaded cache. You might also want to increase the size of caches to handle large media files; you'll need to experiment with this. In Netscape head to **Edit/Preferences** and click **Advanced** to expand it. Select **Cache**. In the menu on the right side of the screen click **Clear Memory Cache** and **Clear Disk Cache**. Click **OK**, then close and reload your browser. In Explorer, select **Internet Options** from the Tools menu and head to the **General** tab. Under **Temporary Internet Files**, click the **Delete Files** button, then click **OK**. Close and reload your browser.

IT'S ABOUT ANIMALS RADIO SHOW
http://itsaboutanimals.com

CALLING ALL PETS RADIO SHOW
http://www.wpr.org/pets/pets.html

"SIT MEANS SIT" RADIO TALK SHOW
http://www.lovemypets.com/sitmeanssit/show.htm

AUDUBON SOCIETY ON THE RADIO
http://www.earthnewsradio.org/naspage.htm

- "Network congestion" errors can mean that a lot of other people are on the Net or that your ISP is overloaded. You may need to try watching (or listening) later in the evening, when there isn't as much traffic on the Web.
- If you get timeout errors, the broadcast server may be overloaded from other users. It may also be because your ISP has heavy traffic.
- If you can't connect to the broadcast server at all, it may be because many other people are trying to tap in. These broadcast sites can only handle a limited number of viewers at once.
- If sound seems distorted, and you're using RealPlayer, tweak it to work more efficiently with your sound card. Pull down the **View** menu and select **Preferences**. Under **Sound Card Compatibility**, click the **Settings** button. Try selecting either "Disable 16-bit sound" or "Disable custom sampling rate," then click **OK**. If the music doesn't sound any better try disabling the other setting. You should also take a look at the **Bandwidth** setting, found in the **Connection** tab, and make sure it's set to the speed of your modem.

CALLING ALL PETS
http://www.wpr.org/pets/carriage.html

A list of radio stations across the United States carrying All Pets.

THE HORSEMAN'S RADIO WEEKLY
WITH JIM CAMPBELL
http://www.HRWNET.com

YAHOO! BROADCAST—ANIMAL TALK RADIO
http://www.animaltalkradio.com

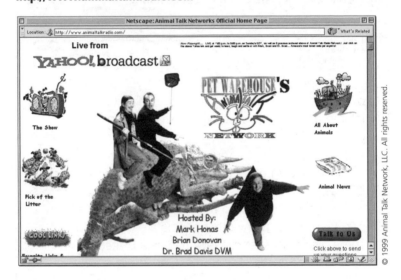

To locate additional talk radio shows that broadcast over the Internet, tap into Broadcast Talk from BroadcastAmerica.com (**http://talk.broadcastamerica.com**).

free Guides to Pet-Friendly Travel

The **American Animal Hospital Association** (**http://www.healthypet.com**) states that 53% of pet owners vacation or travel with their pets. That translates to millions of pooches, cats, and critters on the highways and skyways. The sites in this chapter will help you locate pet-friendly lodging, leash-free parks—even vacation destinations that welcome pets. Be sure to read the travel tips for suggestions such as taking along a photograph of your pet in case it gets lost, having fresh water available for your pet at all times, and stopping regularly to give your pet grass time. The Humane Society of the U.S. reminds us that not all pets are suited for travel because of temperament, illness, or physical impairment. When in doubt, consult your veterinarian.

Web Sites Offering Free Pet-Friendly Travel Guides and Advice

TAKE YOUR PETS
http://www.takeyourpet.com

There's a free travel newsletter you can sign up for and free pet travel guides covering travel tips, car, air, and lodging etiquette. Viewing other areas requires registration and a small membership fee.

TRAVELING WITH YOUR PET
http://www.hsus.org/programs/companion/pet_care/pet_travel.html

The Humane Society of the U.S. offers an assortment of splendid articles for traveling with your pet.

PETS WELCOME
http://www.petswelcome.com

Replete with pertinent pet travel information, Pets Welcome includes a list of pet-friendly venues and classified services for pets and their owners. There are profuse listings to U.S., Canadian, and French lodgings, ski resorts, camp-grounds, beaches, kennels, bed & breakfasts, amusement parks, vacation rentals, and hotel chains. There are even listings to emergency veterinary clinics so you'll know in advance where one is located in the area to which you're heading. Additionally, Pets Welcome is in the process of breaking down the hotels by chains and explaining their overall pet policies and restrictions—if they have any. Also included is a database of pet sitters so you can arrange a sitter not only for your home, but also when on vacation.

INTERPET EXPLORER
http://www.InterPetExplorer.com

Use this site to search for dog-friendly hotels, motels, or pet sitters. Car rental information is coming soon. Be sure to visit the helpful first aid tips page before leaving home.

PET FRIENDLY
http://www.petfriendly.co.uk

Here's a guide to pet-friendly lodging, camping, beaches, and related destinations located throughout the U.K., Ireland, Scotland, Walte, and France.

🛒 THE JET SET PET
http://www.thejetsetpet.com

Staffed by a group of pet travel experts dedicated to simplifying travel with pets, tap into Accommodations for a detailed database of all U.S. hotels that welcome pets, reviews, and a list of pet-friendly hotel/motel chains. Travel Trends features the latest in pet travel news. Resource includes everything from national and state park regulations to international quarantine rules and pet transportation options. Travel tips, pet-oriented destinations, access to pet-travel experts, and many other travel resources are also available.

🛒 TRAVEL PETS
http://www.travelpets.com

Travel Pets features a broad directory to U.S., Canadian, and international pet-friendly hotels.

SAN DIEGO PET.COM
http://www.sandiegopet.com

Beaches, hotels and motels, parks, restaurants, and stores that you and your pet are welcome to visit in the San Diego, California area.

PET VACATIONS
http://www.petvacations.com

A searchable database to pet-friendly motels and hotels.

PETS FROM THE GREAT OUTDOOR RECREATION PAGES
http://www.gorp.com/gorp/eclectic/pets.htm

Historic Hydrants in Washington, D.C., Spots for You and Your Dog in the Florida Keys, and *Traveling Abroad Doggie Style* are some of the friendly, comprehensive articles you'll find at this site. **Travel with Your Pet (http://www2.gorp.com/gorp/trips/spi_pet.asp)** includes a database of trips and tours for you and your pet.

U.S. CUSTOMS TRAVELER INFORMATION— PETS/ANIMALS
http://www.customs.gov/travel/pet.htm

Pets taken out of the United States and returned are subject to the same requirements as those entering for the first time. This site explains U.S. Customs requirements.

AIR TRAVEL FOR YOUR CAT OR DOG
http://www.air-transport.org/public/pets/Default.htm

OK4PETS—MICHIGAN'S PET-FRIENDLY PEOPLE AND PLACES
http://www.ok4pets.com

SAFETY TIPS—TAKING YOUR PET ALONG, FROM THE AMERICAN VETERINARY MEDICAL ASSOCIATION
http://www.avma.org/care4pets/safetrav.htm

There are times when taking along your pet on vacation isn't feasible. If you don't have a relative or friend who can care for your pet while away, and if your pet can't tolerate a kennel, consider a pet sitter. Visit the **National Association of Professional Pet Sitters (http://www.pet sitters.org)**. Enter your zip code, check off the animal type and service desired, and click a button. A list of sitters will appear. Remember to check references before entrusting your pet to anyone.

Web Sites Offering Free Dog-Friendly Travel Advice

DOG LOVERS.COM
http://www.dog-lovers.com

Here's a resource to numerous places to go with your dog, such as parks, beaches, restaurants, hotels, motels, and inns. A directory of pet-related services is also available.

DOG FRIENDLY
http://www.dogfriendly.com

DOG-WALK EVENTS
http://members.aol.com/TesterDesp/walklist.html

ALL THE DOG PARKS IN THE U.S.
http://www.freeplay.org/allparks

🛒 DOGPARK.COM
http://www.dogpark.com

The centerpiece of this easy-to-navigate site is a national directory of off-leash dogparks, organized by state. It also includes dog events, articles, and interviews about a variety of subjects dog lovers will enjoy.

SAFE AIRLINE TRAVEL WITH YOUR DOG, BY DAVID DELEISSEGUES
http://www.dogzone.com/reading/travel.htm

DOG PARKS, DOG RUNS, AND OFF-LEASH PLAY BY DIANE BLACKMAN
http://www.dog-play.com/dogpark.html

📷 DOGS BY THE BAY
http://www.dogsbythebay.com

This e-zine started as a place to inform individuals about places in the Bay Area, in California, one can take their pooch to. It's grown to include recipes, free postcards, and other fun.

🛒 TRAVEL DOG
http://www.traveldog.com

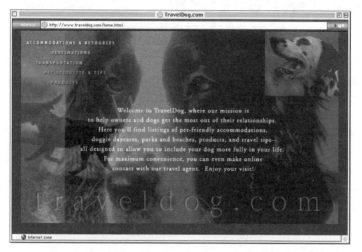

This attractive site includes directories to pet-friendly accommodations, doggie daycares, parks, and beaches. It also includes products, pet etiquette, and travel tips. An online travel agent is available for your convenience.

THE DOG PARK
http://thedogpark.com

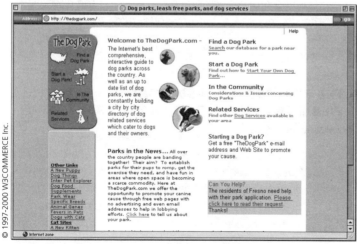

For good reason, this site claims to be the best guide to dog parks across the country. Learn how you can start a park in your area or search for other dog services, like groomers or trainers.

free Pet Loss
Grief Support

The heartbreak and agony we feel when a beloved pet dies or becomes seriously ill can be profound. Sometimes the grief is coupled with guilt when euthanasia or separation is a factor. Only another animal lover can begin to understand the depth of pain you can experience. If you are mourning the loss of a special pet—whether dog, cat, bird, or other living creature—you can obtain emotional support and solace through the Web. While it may seem a lonely place to turn, the words of others who genuinely care and understand your pain are remarkably warm and deeply comforting. They can help you through the healing process.

THE ASSOCIATION FOR PET LOSS AND BEREAVEMENT
http://www.aplb.org

This nonprofit organization is dedicated to assisting people during their pet-mourning process. In addition to offering three weekly live chats, the site includes a state-by-state guide to support groups, counseling centers, pet-bereavement counselors, hotlines, and pet cemeteries and crematories.

THE PET-LOSS GRIEF-SUPPORT WEB SITE & CANDLE CEREMONY
http://www.petloss.com

*Pet Loss welcomes those who are grieving over the death of a pet or an ill pet. You'll find support and thoughtful advice through message boards, a live chat., and heartfelt articles. You also find tribute pages, healing poetry, The Pets Candle Ceremony, and additional related assistance including a directory of pet grief support by telephone (**http://www.petloss.com/phones.htm**) and links to online support groups.*

IN MEMORY OF PETS
http://www.in-memory-of-pets.com

Created by John E. Mingo, Sr. in memory of Candy, John's Cocker Spaniel, this poignant site offers abundant grief support and guidance, pet tributes, a bulletin board, and additional helpful information.

PORTRAIT OF AN ANGEL
http://www.angelbluemist.com

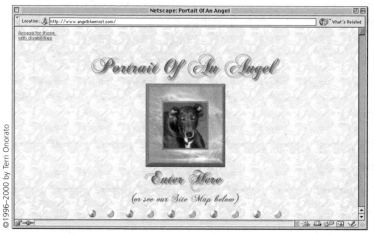

Terri Onorato shares elegant poetry, heartwarming stories, and impassioned guidance in a section called "conversations with guilt."

DOGGIE HEAVEN
http://www.doggyheaven.com.au

Doerthe Jansen created Doggie Heaven as a multi-media project to honor her dog, Cora. She invites you to share your idea of doggie heaven.

LIGHTENING STRIKE PET SUPPORT PAGE
http://www.lightning-strike.com

The goal of this heartfelt site is to provide "lightning-fast" assistance and support for the grieving owners of dead, dying, sick, and missing animals. It offers a pet-loss-support message board, a live chat, links to pet-loss sympathy cards, a link to archives of the alt.support.grief.pet-loss newsgroup, and related guidance.

CORNELL UNIVERSITY PET LOSS SUPPORT LINE
http://web.vet.cornell.edu/Public/petloss

The Pet Loss Support Hotline is staffed by volunteer veterinary students. All e-mail and telephone calls are answered. Additional references, including other hotlines around the country and information on the stages of grieving are included.

SUPER DOG'S PET LOSS—
A REFERENCE TO REFERENCES
http://www.superdog.com/petloss.htm

An excellent collection of resources, including a directory of funeral homes, cemeteries, and memorial markers; a select group of comforting poems and stories; a list of counselors; and information on how you can contribute to a charity or animal rescue organization in your pet's name as a way to keep its memory alive.

DELTA SOCIETY® PET LOSS AND BEREAVEMENT
http://deltasociety.org/dsn000.htm

The Delta Society® promotes the mutually beneficial relationships between animals and people. This page offers a growing collection of resources, including support hotlines, pet-loss Web sites, pet cemeteries and memorials, and pet-loss counselors.

HAVING TO SAY GOODBYE
FROM THE LAND OF PURE GOLD
http://landofpuregold.com/loss.htm

Rochelle Lesser reminds us through story and poem how our pets made our lives better. Toll-free support hotline numbers and resources, such as a collection of books that may offer comfort, are included.

VIRTUAL PET CEMETERY
http://www.mycemetery.com

A place to immortalize your beloved pet.

INDEX

ABOUT THE AUTHOR

Gloria Hansen lives with her husband, dog, and several tropical fish tanks. Her extended family's current menagerie includes five dogs, four cats, a cockateil, two parrots, a cage of finches, a horse, and a ferret. Gloria is the author or co-author of 12 other Internet or computer-related books. She is also an award-winning quiltermaker. Her work—often designed using a Macintosh computer—has appeared in numerous magazines, books, and on television. She has written for leading computer magazines (including *Family Circle* and *PC World*) and craft publications (including *Quilters Newsletter Magazine*, *McCalls Quilting*, and *Art/Quilt Magazine*), and she writes the "High Tech Quilting" column for *The Professional Quilter*. You can visit her Web page at **http://www.gloria-hansen.com**. Gloria lives in East Windsor Township, New Jersey.

For more information on other fine books from C&T Publishing, write for a free catalog:
C&T Publishing, Inc., P.O. Box 1456, Lafayette, CA 94549
(800) 284-1114

http://www.ctpub.com
e-mail: ctinfo@ctpub.com

FREE STUFF ON THE INTERNET SERIES

Frustrated with spending hours of valuable time surfing your way around the Internet? C&T Publishing's Free Stuff on the Internet Series helps you quickly find information on your favorite craft or hobby. Our Free Stuff guides make it easy to stay organized as you visit hundreds of sites that offer all kinds of free patterns, articles, e-mail advice, galleries, and more. This series of handy guides lets you explore the Internet's infinite possibilities.

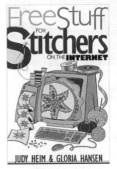

Free Stuff for Stitchers

Includes Web pages for knitters, machine knitters, cross-stitchers, plastic canvas stitchers, beaders, tatters and other lacemakers, spinners, weavers, braiders, knotters, tasselers, and bowmakers. This book is the stitcher's guide to the Internet's infinite possibilities.

Free Stuff for Sewing Fanatics

Includes Web sites that offer free stuff for all kinds of sewing topics, including tailoring and fitting, sewing machine help, upholstery and draperies, home décor sewing, dollmaking, patterns and tutorials, heirloom vintage and bridal sewing, serging, fabric embellishment, and sewing for kids and pets.

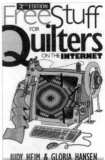

Free Stuff for Quilters, 2nd Edition

The 2nd Edition of Free Stuff for Quilters includes over 150 updated new links on quilt patterns and tips, quilt discussion groups, guilds, and organizations, plus quilt shops to visit when you travel, how-tos for fabric dyeing, painting, stamping, photo transferring, and galleries of quilts, textiles, and fiber arts.

www.ctpub.com